Slow River

Steve Strevens

ALLEN&UNWIN

First published in 2006

Copyright © Steve Strevens 2006

Map by Ian Faulkner

Allen & Unwin
83 Alexander Street
Crows Nest NSW 2065
Australia
Phone: (61 2) 8425 0100
Fax: (61 2) 9906 2218
Email: info@allenandunwin.com
Web: www.allenandunwin.com

National Library of Australia
Cataloguing-in-Publication entry:

Strevens, Steve.
Slow River.

ISBN 978 1 74114 986 9

ISBN 1 74114 986 X.

1. Murray River (N.S.W.-S. Aust.) - Description and travel.
I. Title.

919.44

Typeset in 11.5/15 Bembo by Midland Typesetters, Victoria
Printed in Australia by Griffin Press, Adelaide

10 9 8 7 6 5 4 3 2 1

Foreword

The Murray is a slow river. It is said that it drops only one inch every couple of kilometres on its epic journey to the sea. It doesn't run fast towards its destiny—which of late it can't fulfil anyway—other than when it races from the mountains into Lake Hume, which imprisons it, and just after, when the huge walls of the weir are lowered slightly to liberate the river in small doses. Yet the Murray is powerful, with its great mass of slow water generating great hydraulic pressure and strength.

Billabongs are the visual representations of that strength. The river slowly works to cut its way short, and once that's achieved it tries to create yet another. It may take a century or two before the river breaks through and you are never there to witness it. That's a slow river.

As a member of the International Slow Food Movement, an organisation that stands against all things fast, especially food, I appreciate the power of slowness. I share this appreciation with Steve Strevens who is aware of the parallel between 'slow' as a river quality as well as the 'slow' food movements. When Steve embarks on his journey down the Murray, he becomes almost part of the river, physically and emotionally embracing both notions of 'slow' which is the ultimate gaol of this philosophy.

Slow River is Steve's evocative exploration of this country's great waterway. It is sensitive, thoughtful and captivating; a personal and intimate reflection which slowly creeps up on the reader. Steve takes you along on his journey and manages to celebrate the river without succumbing to the usual 'mighty Murray' clichés.

New York poet and scholar Paul Kane, who has had a long association with Australia and the Murray, wrote a poem about our river in 1995. It has not been published anywhere to my knowledge but I think it belongs in this book. The poem anticipates many of the themes of Steve's story. It is also far more eloquent than anything further I'd have to say.

On the Murray, Mildura 1995

Rising from heights rare in Australia, the Murray uncoils
like a great serpent on a journey cross country, the long
line traversing, composing, all terrains—as if limming
the borders of at least three states of mind: call them the New,
the South and the Victorian. The Murray's capaciousness
is legendary, and the flow, like the great poem endless in its
variations and surety. In America, we'd
call the Murray the Mississippi, but only a blues
player and Brodsky's cat are famous for it. Rivers are
like that: you never know who they are going to invoke.
The Murray, a river of work, cutting its way through time
and all resistance: here broad and reflecting, there deep and
gorgeous in confinement—scoriated limestone valleys
of imagination—and stillness too, in swampy
backwaters and billabongs, where the traveller, the river's
reader, can paddle about and muse on the curious
vicissitudes of Nature's Muse, who is also like a
river, only she is her own source of plenishment,
whereas the Murray—refreshed by loss—is both less and more.

Stefano De Pieri

Contents

Prologue

I was eleven years old in the summer of 1959, the year the Murray River flowed quietly into my soul.

At once strong, wide and mysterious, it seemed dangerous and yet friendly and gentle as well. Sitting with my back against a tall, ancient tree I gazed across the water. The gum trees on the opposite bank waved gently in the hot summer breeze as the strange creaking call of black and white birds floated through the air. I didn't know it then but no matter what happened to me later, the river would always be with me.

The river that was to become such a powerful, evocative presence in my life was very different from the rivers in Cambridgeshire, England, where I was born. Only a few small rivers graced the flat expanses of the Fens, together with the many canals that had been dug by hand from as far back as Roman times to drain the area. Fishing these was a favourite pastime.

Not far from our village was Cambridge, with its famously picturesque river, offering idyllic postcard views of punting on the Cam, and long languid picnics under oak trees with beautiful girls in white cotton dresses and straw hats. Not that I took much notice of them, being a mere boy, intent more on cricket and football than poetry or romance. But the peculiar charm of the Fens and the enchanting river Cam were to become distant memories—Dad had decided we should emigrate to Australia.

We came to the country. Dad said that cities were all much the same and he wanted to go to the 'real Australia'. Besides, the job that went with being part of the 'Bring Out a Briton' program was on a fruit block in the Riverland of South Australia, at a little place called Glossop.

On the day our ship docked in Adelaide, the man Dad was to work for collected my parents, myself and my three siblings, together with a collection of battered tea-chests filled with all our worldly possessions, and drove us four hours to our new home. For us kids it was a fascinating adventure but, many years later, Dad—a World War II veteran—admitted that he had never been more scared in his life than when standing on that wharf.

We settled in as much as was possible in such an alien land. We lived in an old weatherboard house a mile from the township. There were snakes and lizards in the garden during the day as well as all manner of strange noises at night. The heat was stifling and the hot north wind kept me awake all night as it whistled and howled through the flywire walls in the sleepout. We had arrived during one of the hottest summers ever. With temperatures regularly touching 40 degrees, it was hotter than I could have ever imagined.

One day Dad's boss took us to Berri, a larger town a short distance away, and as the others shopped and talked, I wandered off. Two streets away, I found the river. I sat transfixed on the bank, fingering the coarse grass and watching the water as it flowed past, wondering where it had come from, and where it was going. How different it was from the water I had been used to. There would be no dainty, pale-skinned beauties here, only strong women with hands toughened by work. This was a place for the wide-brimmed hats that I'd seen men wearing, not straw boaters. And what sort of fish swam deep under the barely noticeable ripples? Surely not the tench and carp of England. No, these would be real fighting fish, huge and edible.

Scuffing at a few stones, I slouched back towards the shops along streets that had peppercorn trees on the verges and geranium and rosemary bushes growing ruggedly near the small wire fences. I didn't want to leave the river. Even though I didn't know quite how to describe it, there was something about it that made me feel, well, *good*.

That night, in fitful sleep, I dreamt about the river, with myself as a sort of Australian friend of Huckleberry Finn, travelling wherever the river travelled, with only the birds and the fish for company, and the current as my guide.

We soon moved into Berri, exchanging the isolation of our first home for neighbours and a yard full of cats and dogs. Best of all, around the corner and across the football ground was the Murray.

The river entranced me. There was an unknown freedom on its banks; hours spent fishing and listening to the wind in the trees or hearing the aerodynamic swoosh as birds swooped through the air around me. The more time I spent near the river, the more I dreamt. I promised myself that one day I would go and see the rest of it.

A couple of years later we moved further upstream into Victoria, where life continued in much the same way. In summer I would swing out and plunge into the river on ropes secured by boys like me who scrambled precariously along the branches of the overhanging trees; I fished and swam in its waters, camped on its banks and pretended that its sandbars were beaches.

Three weeks after my sixteenth birthday I left home to join the navy, but on each leave I would return to be renewed again, thirsting for what I missed. Ten years later I returned for good.

As life rolled inexorably by, family, work and sport made my trips to the river more infrequent, although I still managed to see it at least three times a week. Even a few minutes watching the water or a walk in the silence of the red gums was enriching. During those years my desire to see the river in its entirety became stronger. I wanted to savour the river over a year, to see the changes in the people and the land through the seasons. I decided to make my journey by tinnie, when possible, but also to canoe and to travel in a houseboat. I wanted to find out what people who live along the river think about the many problems it faces. And from farmers to fishermen, tourists to paddle-steamer captains, I wanted to talk to the people who use and love the river to find out what it means to them.

I knew the river had changed since first we met. It seemed that of the millions of years it had existed the last twenty had been the worst; pollution had become more obvious and irrigation had increased dramatically. In that time the world had also changed, I had changed. The prospect of discovering how was intriguing.

The song of the river ends not at her banks, but in the hearts of those who have loved her.

Buffalo Joe

The mark of a successful man is one that has spent an entire day on the bank of a river without feeling guilty about it.

Chinese Philosopher

The care of rivers is not a question of rivers, but of the human heart.

Tanaka Shozo

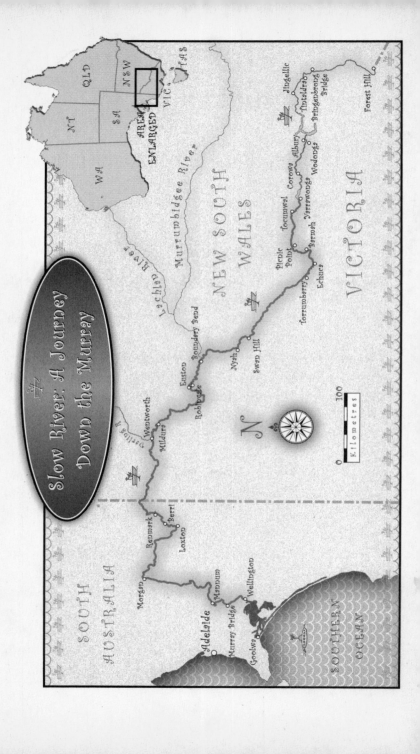

Midsummer

The Mountain to Bringenbrong

I was disappointed. I had expected more. This was not how a mighty river should begin. It should have been clean and green and luxuriant, a babbling brook, a spring of clear water. A place where I could feel the spirit of beginning, the complexity of a million years.

Instead, after a few squishing steps, there behind stumpy, twisted tea-trees high up on this mountain, a swampy puddle oozed brackishly through the matted undergrowth. A metre-high piece of galvanised pipe stuck in the ground was all that marked the place. How demeaning.

My companion smiled in amusement at my reaction. Richard Hubbard had been here many times.

Middle-aged, balding and with a beard speckled with grey, Richard, with his wife Sandra, ran a bed and breakfast at Corryong named, appropriately, Old Mother Hubbard's. They had moved from the city some twenty years before, with Richard teaching at the local school before establishing both the

B & B and a business catering for people wanting to see the high country.

The previous night we had sat on his verandah in the warm mid-January air while he told me what to expect. The trip to the source of the Murray wasn't, Richard explained, as simple as I might have thought. A three-hour drive over the mountains and into the national park would be followed by an eight-hour walk—four in and four out. We would then camp overnight before heading back.

In the early hours of the next morning, Richard's four-wheel drive spluttered into life, and we soon left the safety of the main road and headed into the bush.

As much as the journey was long, it was also steep. As we bounced and battered our way up the mountain, Richard explained how he and a few others had set up a community education system for older folk in Corryong. They attracted volunteer tutors who suggested that, in return, he could use his four-wheel drive to take people up into the mountains occasionally. Thus his business was born.

We were heading through the Kosciuszko National Park on a track that had been put in when the Snowy Mountains Hydro-Electric Scheme commenced, to provide access between the town of Khancoban and Tom Groggin, the cattle station which ran alongside the Murray. Contrary to popular belief, Tom Groggin was not named after a famous local identity, but comes from the Aboriginal word 'tomarogin' meaning 'water spider'.

As well as plenty of potholes and fallen trees, there were, remarkably, speed humps every few hundred metres. The track was still used regularly. Although men and women on horseback shifted most of the cattle around the mountains, there were still supplies to get through, timber to be removed, and the odd few cattle to be moved in trucks. How they did it in the early days, before the advent of the track, was difficult to comprehend; even now it was hard enough with the fallen rocks and branches littering the way, together with overhanging ferns and the twists and turns of the road.

Stringybarks, some rendered dark and mysterious by the fires that had swept through the High Country almost three years earlier, were plentiful. They bore a strange look of regeneration; some were green, some were brown but many were still black. Light streamed eerily through their branches making shadows like twisted fingers that quickly disappeared as the clouds rolled on. The sun's rays cut slits through the mists in the valleys and shone on the ferns. In the distance, the summits of two mountains disappeared into clouds. 'That's Townsend and Kosciuszko,' said Richard. 'Beautiful, aren't they?'

Ten minutes later we nosedived around a corner and headed down the Geehi Walls, famed, Richard mentioned needlessly, for their steepness. Easing down the hill in low gear, he told me a story about a cattle farmer who, many years before, had become bogged going up the Walls with a truck full of his beasts. He headed off on foot to find a bulldozer to tow him out and while he was away the cattle started stamping impatiently. The result was the truck slowly but surely sliding back down the mountain.

Looking out of the window at the valleys thousands of feet below, I could see water sparkling and flashing before disappearing into the dense forest. This was the country of the Wolgal people. Their neighbours, the Yaitmathang, were closer to Corryong. Before the white man came, other mountain clans joined these tribes at winter's end for the annual bogong feasting. Food was scarce during the cold months and bogong moths were a delicacy. The tribes gathered at a place they called Jagungal, where they'd smoke the moths from their hiding places and capture them in skins and nets. They would eat so much they'd become ill then, after recovering, make their way back to their own lands. In 1836, when squatters with sheep and cattle came to look for new grazing land at the foot of the mountains and for water in the river, the gatherings became less and less frequent. By 1862 there were only four full-blooded survivors of the Wolgal people.

At Buckwong Creek we stopped and listened to the rush of the water as it tumbled headlong over the rocks on its way to join the Murray. The sun filtered through the cobwebs, picking out spiders on the stringybarks.

'That means there's some rain around,' Richard informed me. He pointed to a flock of black cockatoos swarming over-head. 'When they're around and the springs are running and the ants are building little hills, it'll rain.'

From here we climbed the Silks, on a fire track that spiralled like the stripe on a barber's pole and loose soil shifted repeatedly under the wheels. The valley was now on the right-hand side, a sheer drop from just beside the tyres through the mountain ash to almost certain death.

Higher up the mountain the timber changed to alpine ash, their long tentacle-like branches, unaffected by the fires, reaching through the sunlight as we battled our way onwards at an almost 45-degree angle. Around one corner we suddenly dropped into a crater caused by the washaway from heavy rain. Luckily Richard was prepared for such eventualities, and I was sent up the track carrying a chain that Richard pulled out from the winch on the Land Rover. He then joined me and hooked it round the sturdiest tree he could find before winching us back to safer ground.

At Charlie's Creek a flock of gang-gangs screeched at us while further on a fallen tree with a few sheets of corrugated iron attached served as yards for the cattlemen's dogs. Charlie's Creek was named a hundred years ago after a stockman whose packhorse decided to head off and join the brumbies, leaving him stranded. It is said that Charlie, whose surname no one remembers, perished nearby.

By the time we reached 1800 metres, the ash had given way to snow gums—with their glistening patches of creamy bark, stunted growth, small leaves and mossy branches, it was like driving through a fairytale forest. Half an hour later, Richard pulled up beside the Moscow Creek entrance to Cobberas National Park. It was time for the four-hour walk.

The first 500 metres were uphill but, thankfully, after that the terrain flattened for a while. It was slightly humid but not cold or hot, a strange feeling for the middle of summer. Back at Corryong the temperature was expected to reach 35 degrees. At home in Swan Hill it was going to be about 40. Yet here the mid-afternoon felt like dusk, with the light fading early and the night air sweeping in. Along the track were plenty of brumby droppings and every now and again a wallaby would burst from the scrub, bouncing erratically, dodging imaginary objects. Richard said that when the snow gums became much thicker we would be near the top. Grimly, I noted they were still three metres apart.

Thirty minutes later we turned off the track. The gums were so close now that occasionally we had to turn sideways to get through. The forest floor was a mat of rotting trees and new native grasses, but dotted throughout were small heads of pink mountain flowers that brought an unexpected colour and gentleness to the rugged environment.

It took us an hour or more to move a few hundred metres. As I battled through, pushing aside branches and feeling my feet crunch through the timber beneath me, I knew what Stanley must have felt like when he was chasing Livingstone in Africa all those years ago.

'Not long now,' Richard called over his shoulder. I was glad of that, ever mindful that if we had an accident we could be there a thousand years and never heard from again. Besides, whippy wattles were stinging my legs as we flipped through them and hungry March flies took turns to pick at my face. I didn't have enough arms to deal with both.

Ten minutes later we entered a small clearing on the slope of Forest Hill. A moss-covered stone cairn has sat there for over a century, built in 1870 by the surveyors Alexander Black and Alexander Allen. It was the first in a series that went in a straight line to Cape Howe on the coast—which we now recognise as the dotted line on maps that signifies the border of New South Wales and Victoria. I wondered what the men were thinking as they looked out over the mountains at the country they would have to cross to reach the sea.

Richard interrupted my thoughts to explain that technically the source of the Murray is the spring closest to the cairn. He turned away, ducked under some tea-tree bushes and there was the galvanised pipe.

My disappointment clutched at me. I had expected to marvel at the beginning of an icon; to think about how, millions of years ago, this was where the river began its journey to Goolwa, thousands of kilometres away—but all I could see was squelchy rotten water and a pipe.

Yet there was something intangible on top of that mountain. The breeze was slight and cool in my hair; the silence punctuated only by the occasional cry of a bird and the rustle of the wind in the trees. A minute or so later Richard's voice broke the stillness. 'Come on,' he said. 'This'll make you feel better.'

A hundred metres away my whole mood changed. For there it was, filtering down the mossy mountain: a steady stream of pure, clean water, shimmering its way through the small mounds and around the ancient, gnarled roots of trees.

I stood with one foot in Victoria and the other in New South Wales, leaned down, cupped my hand and drank. And even though it tasted horrible, all the dreams I'd ever had about the river surged through me along with the water. There are things you look forward to so much that they seldom live up to expectations. But this was different. Richard said many people thought they had travelled the Murray but really hadn't. He was right. Unless you'd seen this place, the source, you'd not seen the Murray.

We began to walk, observing how gently, softly, the small creek gradually widened as it tumbled over the outcrops made by the brumbies. The stream became wider and deeper with each step and, despite the river's edge being crushed by the wild horses and grazing cattle, and their pollution being washed into the water, I still felt a sense of awe; a sense of what was, and what was to come.

As much as possible we followed the river back to the campsite, arriving exhausted, a few hours later. We pitched the tent and built a campfire, then Richard cooked and we opened a bottle of wine. A billion stars covered the sky like a sparkling lid and the moon, round and fat, seemed very close at hand.

The early morning silence was broken as a few brumbies that had wandered near the camp thundered off when something disturbed them. We packed up and drove towards Surveyor's

Creek, one of numerous creeks and small rivers that contributed their water to the Murray. As we parked and, on foot, headed once more through the scrub, I wondered how far it would be this time. Fortunately, we emerged after only a few minutes at a spot where the creek was about ten metres wide.

A large tree—mossy, damp and treacherous-looking—led to the opposite bank. Richard took the first steps. On reaching the centre he almost overbalanced, his arms flailing wildly in circles as he struggled to recover his equilibrium before finishing the journey. I studied the tree for a minute then inched my way to the middle before taking three huge strides that landed me safely on the other side. Twenty metres away was a pile of rocks that at one time was a chimney, and holes in the ground where posts for walls once stood. Richard called me over to a small plaque that he and a few others had placed there in 1995.

Jack Riley, the man from Snowy River died here July 14, 1914

For over thirty years, Jack Riley had worked at Tom Groggin, living in a log cabin on the New South Wales side of the river. He was known as the Hermit of Tom Groggin and, because of his abilities as a stockman, bushman and horseman, was said to have been the model for Banjo Paterson's 'The Man from Snowy River'. Indeed, Paterson visited him at least twice to drink whisky and listen to his stories.

Advancing years and the rough bush life resulted in health problems for Riley, but he refused to leave the mountains for treatment. When his condition worsened, friends loaded him onto a stretcher and took turns carrying him through the scrub to Corryong Hospital. The track over the mountains consisted of not much more than rocks and the men soon found the task of walking and carrying a stretcher at the same time beyond them. They sat Riley on his horse, tied him upright, and the smallest and lightest man climbed on behind to steady him. Two others walked alongside holding him in place.

Snow began to fall but they pushed on. Once over the top of the mountain they placed him back on the stretcher and reached the spot where we now sat, the remains of a tin miner's hut. Here they stopped and made him comfortable by sitting him near a fire. Riley rallied during the night but shortly afterwards the heart that had carried him through all his adventures gave out. He was eighty-seven years of age.

My mind was still on Jack Riley when we made our way very carefully back across the tree bridge, leaving his ghosts to the quiet.

The river appeared periodically on our journey back to Corryong. Each time it was wider and stronger. Suddenly, we were out of the bush and back on bitumen. Back in the real world with no bumping beneath the feet, no crashing or bashing, just open space, powerlines, traffic on the roads, advertising billboards in paddocks, and the hum of rubber on the tar.

I didn't see the river closely again until we crossed the Bringenbrong Bridge outside Corryong. We got out of the car and walked to the middle of the bridge, silently studying the water as it surged exuberantly below us, some 2500 kilometres away from its destination.

Back at Old Mother Hubbard's, I thanked Richard for giving me an understanding of where I was going by showing me where my river had come from.

Throwing my backpack into the ute I drove off with the window down, contentedly basking in the summer wind that was blowing down from the mountains.

Late summer

Bringenbrong to Hume Dam

Early one Sunday, a month after my excursion with Richard, I launched my tinnie at the Bringenbrong Bridge.

The small aluminium boat slipped with a gurgle into the water and I gingerly stepped aboard. After a couple of pulls the outboard coughed into life. Taking my place on a plastic garden chair without legs, secured to a swivelling fixture, it occurred to me that this was not the best or most comfortable of seats for a long voyage. Hopefully, the small cushion would help soften the connection between backside and plastic.

As the sun rose higher, shadows from trees that earlier had stretched intermittently across the river began to disappear. In the open areas I could see almost to the bottom through the clean water but in the darker places, although still clear, the water swirled secretively. Changing sporadically from wide to narrow, the river's banks were full of trees on the bends yet bare when it straightened. There was no other river traffic and there were no other people on the banks, it was just me, the mountain views, the delicate white clouds, and the gargling sound of a slow-revving outboard motor. My journey proper had begun.

By now the Murray had started its course westward after flowing north for the first 250 kilometres. It had dropped some 1600 metres in altitude in that time and was about to become one of the slowest rivers in the world, but the current was still reasonably swift here and it wasn't long before I arrived at Towong.

The Towong Racing Club was on the other side of town, not far from the river—but then nothing in the town was. The club was formed in 1871 and scenes from the movie *Phar Lap* had been filmed at the racecourse. The steps of the grandstand—a rare combination of wrought iron, wood and imagination—creaked under my feet. Sitting on the wooden seats and staring across the track, I could almost hear the thunder of distant hooves and the shouts of the crowds.

The famous larrikin crook Squizzy Taylor also visited the club. In 1928 he and his gang turned up, created an almighty disturbance as a distraction, and stole a heap of money. Not content with that, Squizzy and his mates also stopped at Corryong and robbed the local pub.

There was still no one on the river when I returned to the boat, apart from a solitary figure who sat on a fold-up chair carefully baiting a hook. He didn't seem to notice me, or at least didn't acknowledge my presence. I decided against wandering up. If it were me, I would have preferred to be left to throw in my line in peace.

Amongst the assorted items in the boat was a small battery-powered radio. The clearest station was the ABC, and as I chugged along, suddenly the air was filled with Delibes' 'Flower Duet'. Cutting the motor and using a paddle to guide the drifting boat, I immersed myself in the sound, two soaring, quivering female voices and a symphony orchestra; the sound of the voices submerged me in the river's gentle operatic lilt. But soon enough the music finished and it was back to reality. Three hours later, sore backside, crook back and all, I arrived at Tintaldra.

Tintaldra was settled around 1837. It was said that Rowland Shelley, the first local landowner in the district, was a descendant of the English poet Percy Bysshe Shelley.

The main street of Tintaldra—actually, it was the only street—was some 50 metres from where I'd pulled in under the bridge. Beyond the pub, which had a garage attached to it, and the tearooms and general store opposite, there was nothing. Tossing up where to go first, I decided on the tearooms. The floorboards creaked under my feet, which caused the elderly lady reading at one of the tables to look up.

'What can I do for you?' she inquired, smiling and closing her book.

I smiled back and ordered tea.

'Stranger here,' she said, more of a statement than a question.

I studied the building as she attended to my order. The front wall was made from wooden panels while the roof was held up by what had once been huge red gum tree trunks, hewn roughly by hand into some sort of a square. The interior walls were pressed metal and on them, in an alcove, was a display of local history. I ran my hands over one of the uprights and along the wooden panels.

'Red stringybarks,' came a voice from behind as the woman placed my order a couple of tables away from where she was sitting. Protocol, I presumed. Either that or a hot day in a boat had had another effect on me!

Betty Walton had left Sydney for Tintaldra thirty years previously, becoming a local historian as well as a bush poet who had won many awards at the Man from Snowy River Festival held annually in Corryong. Betty was the author of a short self-published book which, among other things, told of how the town was the first to be settled on the Upper Murray and how it had a hand-hauled punt before the bridge was built.

Betty suggested a tour of her property which backed onto the river. We started at the old bakery, where the ovens still sat impassively in the brick wall. Betty explained the method bakers used to heat the bricks, the way the dampers worked and how she was pleased that all the utensils and the ovens had been built by hand in a Melbourne forge. Her contribution to environmental conservation was next. She pointed to the willow trees lining the opposite bank of the river a little upstream.

'Basket willows,' she said. 'They planted them for the Snowy Scheme, said they would preserve the riverbank on the bends—but they were wrong. They multiply so rapidly they have become absolute pests; they're water suckers, native birds hate them and they drop all their leaves into the water.'

Betty had asked for the trees on her bank to be removed because they had almost reached her backyard. When her request was refused she hired a couple of bulldozers and had it done herself. 'Then I planted some native trees.' She pointed to a group of strong healthy young gum trees. 'I made my own little wetlands area.'

'Is the condition of the Murray as bad as some say it is?' I asked as we stood and watched three ducks splash around, the sound of their antics carrying easily to us.

'Downstream it is,' Betty answered, 'where it is poisoned and dragged out beyond its capacity. But here it's young and vibrant and when the snow melts and the river floods it is magnificent.'

There were six people in the bar at the pub; two leather-clad touring motorcyclists whose machines were parked out the front, three young local blokes wearing big hats, and the barman.

Alf Wilson, arms bearing faded tattoos, welcomed me. He and his wife had run the pub—the first one on the Murray—for sixteen years. Alf had become a publican after giving up his job in a transport company based in Melbourne's western suburbs.

'This beats West Footscray, mate,' he said, shrugging his shoulders to the question of why.

Warning me about wasps getting in my beer, he placed the coaster on top instead of underneath my glass. The local boys wanted refilling so while Alf tended to them I studied the large mounted moose head on the wall. The moose's antlers were covered in cobwebs and its fur had seen better days but he still looked down ceremoniously on the proceedings.

'Funny,' Alf continued with a grin after he returned. 'People staying here reckon they've never had a better-tasting cup of tea but all the water comes straight from the river.'

The river was the lifeblood of the small town, and both Betty and Alf had similar business problems. Local trade had dropped significantly as farms were sold and people moved away, but because of tourists wanting to see the Upper Murray, passing trade had grown almost as much—but it was a much less reliable source of income, varying from season to season.

Alf was also upset about what he considered was water wastage. With a shake of his head he told me that although we are the driest continent on earth, we still grow rice and cotton. 'They need the most water and we have only got it in rivers which are drying up. Doesn't make much sense.'

I finished my beer and left.

That night I camped, lying on top of my swag and hoping the mosquitoes kept away. I stared at the stars and wondered about sleep, but for only a minute.

I had arranged for my ute and boat trailer to be waiting for me in Jingellic, and sure enough there it was, parked under the trees on a naturally flat, spacious camping ground on the river bank. Scattered around were camps of varying size; small tents holding two people, larger ones with families. There was even a motorbike with a sidecar parked next to a pink tent. In the middle of it all, somewhat out of place, was a large American style Winnebago with blue and white paintwork.

Under a willow tree towards one end of the camping ground a boat had been hauled halfway up the bank. Sitting near the motor a fisherman cast and retrieved his line continually. He flicked the line out, saw the plop, waited for a second or two then reeled it in. Then he did it again; and again and again. Monotonous and relaxing.

'Any luck?' I asked.

'With fish?' he responded. 'Nah, but I'm lucky bein' here.'

A flight of fifty or so brick steps had been cut into the hill at the rear of the camping ground. At the top was the Bridge Hotel. The bridge had moved though. One of the old steel pylons rising incongruously from the middle of the river was all that remained. The new bridge was downstream a short distance, which put the pub, now secluded and private, a bit out of the way—a good thing, perhaps.

I ordered a beer at the corner of the bar. The drinker closest to me nodded in my direction and asked what I was up to. After explaining my journey he nodded again and sipped his beer. 'Where've you bin so far?'

My answer was greeted by an exclamation from behind.

'That's all bullshit!' said Andrew Miller, a long-time resident of the area who worked part time at the pub. A small man, he was dressed in a denim shirt and jeans and puffed, almost indignantly, on a pipe while regarding me with suspicion. 'The Murray doesn't start there,' he went on, emphatically. 'That's bullshit. It starts where the Indi and the Swampy Plains meet, just near the Bringenbrong Bridge. All the bloody greenies and them reckon it starts up the top there but it bloody starts at Bringenbrong, that's where. That might be one start of the Murray but Bringenbrong is where it *really* starts.' Andrew finished his beer, shook my hand and left. Although he smiled, he knew I was a disbeliever.

As Andrew walked out, the bloke next to me stuck out his hand. Solidly built with a head full of grey tousled hair, even at nearly seventy, Rex Beaver spoke with a considered air.

Rex had lived in the district for over fifty years. He worked on the Snowy Mountains Scheme for a while, building dams up around Geehi, Jindabyne and Khancoban, before turning his hand to shearing. He'd also worked for the Water Commission as part of a team 'snagging' the river, taking dead trees out of the river to allow a faster flow.

'Went faster orright,' he laughed. 'Started to erode the banks it went so fast.'

Then trees were planted to protect the bank—the willows that Betty Walton hated.

'Why was Andrew so upset?' I asked.

'Don't worry about him,' said Rex. 'As far as the locals are concerned the Murray starts where those two rivers meet but we don't get upset, everyone just has their opinion. Anyway, it's just the most beautiful place on earth and that's all that matters.'

Rex was born in the English midlands and at sixteen saw a Chips Rafferty movie that impressed him so much he announced to his parents he wanted to go to Australia. He made his way to Australia House in London where he was told about the Big Brotherhood movement, an organisation that sponsored young people from England to work in Australia. Eventually Rex arrived in Sydney and was sent to a training farm at Cabramatta, where he learnt simple farming techniques like milking cows and 'a bit about tractors and the like'. A short time later he was given a railway ticket to Albury, from where the young English kid began work on a dairy farm with about fifty cows.

'Talmalmo,' Rex said, 'just eight miles down the river from here.'

He remembered jumping out of the truck, looking around, and saying to himself that God must have had a plan, to lead him to such a beautiful place. 'Even now, it's pristine 'round here, as clear as you can get it. One day it won't be, but at the moment it's magic. Eventually people will come here and stuff it up like they have everywhere else, but hopefully that's long after I've gone.'

The sound of an axe cutting wood split the morning air. Near the river a man and his son stood talking while at another camp a group sat around their fire staring silently at the ground. Everything was peaceful.

Rex had told me that the river downstream was very shallow in places and, as dragging the boat off the riverbed would take more energy than could be mustered, driving was the easiest option.

The low mountain range rose imperiously behind the paddocks along the Murray River Road. Cows, waiting to be milked, stood contentedly, occasionally raising their heads to check out what was passing before returning to munch on the abundant grass. Signs of autumn were apparent. The deciduous trees were changing. Greens becoming browns, scarlet or yellow. All the while the native trees stayed the same.

At the foot of the hills the river wound through the land-scape, almost cutting back on itself in some areas. I tried to imagine the first trickle of water making its way around each obstacle in its path. Many millions of years before there was no river. Then, gradually, there was.

A few kilometres later I drove into the Burrowye Reserve. A sign at the gate warned of strong currents and deep water in places. The boat trailer lurched as I negotiated a few holes but the ground soon flattened out and I backed down to the water's edge. An elderly couple watched with interest from their camp as I struggled to pull the boat off the trailer while also keeping the motor from becoming stuck in the mud. The old bloke wandered down.

'Here,' he instructed, 'you lift and I'll pull.'

Soon the boat was launched and floated on the end of my rope, but not wanting to appear rude, I committed to the conversation.

We stood, enjoying the morning sun, while one of those small, woolly, irritating dogs sat on a camp chair yapping crazily. He had a cover on him, a sort of dog blanket. According to Bill, Fluffy had gone for a walk earlier that morning and fallen in the river. Then, added Marj, the poor little tyke was feeling cold and wanted to get into their bed on his return. Bill and Marj took turns rubbing Fluffy while Fluffy stared at me. They were from Sydney and spent a couple of weeks on the river each year.

'We want to hear nothing,' said Bill, 'and that's what we hear.'

'And it's not only the noise, it's the air,' Marj nodded in agreement. 'We test ourselves out, too. We can get away from each other in the city but not here.' She laughed as she looked at Bill. 'He's not bad, though. I've had him for forty years so a few more won't hurt me.'

They promised to keep an eye on the ute for me, even though the likelihood of anyone stealing it was remote. They waved as I puttered away, the steady surge of the motor causing small waves to slap at the side of the boat.

Once around the bend, when the sound of Fluffy's incessant yapping diminished, I slowed down and wondered if the river would let me float. It didn't. I tried various acrobatic manouvres to allow me to steer with the motor handle while lying down. I didn't expect it to work, it was just that with the sun and the stillness it would have been nice to wallow. Instead I slowed right down until the motor was just gurgling and the boat barely moving.

That worked for a while, but then the motor stalled and wouldn't start again, no matter how much persuasion was used or in what form. Talking nicely, swearing, the odd thump with a spanner, none of it worked; it just drifted into the bank. Leave it alone was the best thing to do, I decided, and go for a walk.

The bank was flat on my side with small gum trees and melaleucas as well as other native shrubbery. The opposite bank was slightly higher. Along it were rows and rows of poplars, as well as a few pine trees, with nary a native tree in sight. When I turned back the view of the river turned with me.

Things always look different from other angles. Take trains for instance. Drive along the roads and you always see the front yards of houses, places that are mostly spick and span. Trains take you behind the scenes. This was similar. Not that there were any backyards, but even the river bends changed everything. The flow of the water, the way the branches and the leaves came off the trees. I doubted anyone would understand this strange reflection on the river but at least it occupied my mind.

The boat was still where I'd left it, thank goodness, and started with the first pull. It, too, might have needed a bit of peace and quiet.

When I returned Marj and Bill told me they had the billy on. In this case the billy was a silver teapot on a gas stove, not a blackened tin thing like mine with dents and a handle that threatened to come off at any minute. Fluffy was dry and a lot calmer. Only a quiet growl and a raised head indicated he had seen me. As Marj handed me a floral cup I asked if they'd ever been further downstream.

'Not really,' said Bill. 'We've heard all about it but this is just so wonderful we don't want to see anything that's spoiled.'

Marj watched while Bill and I made the boat secure on the trailer.

'Enjoy yourself, take care,' they called out as I headed off.

I studied the river through the ute window while at the same time negotiating the bends and trying to keep to my side of the road. Wending its way through green paddocks the narrow river had an almost European appearance with the rolling hills, the mountains behind, and the many species of trees lining its banks.

Around one bend I drove into Wild Dog Valley, according to a sign made from two large slabs of wood a couple of metres high. The words 'Wild Dog Valley' were burnt into the wood and hanging from the cross piece were the remains of nine dogs, their legs tied together with baling twine of varying colours. There was green twine, red, black, yellow and even pink. One dog was nearly a skeleton while a couple of the others seemed quite fresh. The heat of the day accentuated the stink and all the carcasses were covered with flies.

A four-wheel drive stopped at a paddock gate and an arm emerged from the window, catching my attention. It was Peter Sutherland, an older bloke I had met briefly in the Jingellic pub. He had been to an auction that day and seen a 300-acre parcel of land at Thologolong, where his family had been farming for over a hundred years, sold for over a million dollars. Not that Peter had an interest in the property, he just wanted to be there, as most farmers do when land around them is being sold.

Peter was a talkative man. Mid-seventies, I guessed, and wearing a hat which, although wide brimmed, was flat on top and distinguished his age and good taste in headwear.

'Been following a dog but lost him,' he said when I mentioned the sign and asked if it served as a warning to other dogs. He laughed. 'Not sure they take much notice of it, although you'd think they would, some of 'em are that smart.'

Peter's house was on the side of a large hill and we adjourned there for morning tea, served with a large squelchy chocolate cake he'd baked the previous night.

The Sutherland family had emigrated from Scotland in 1852. They ran a few dairy cows among the beef herds, as his grand-mother was the only source of medical care in the area and needed milk sometimes when she made house calls.

'Wild bloody cattle they were in those days,' said Peter. 'They had to rope 'em and pull 'em into the dairy.'

My laughter caused Peter to walk outside and return with an ancient lasso. 'This one's seven-ply rawhide. It'd pull the Queen Mary in but that's what they had to do, about eight or ten a day.'

Peter's family bred Murray Grey cattle, one of the most famous of breeds, with the first one arriving in 1905. 'Happened just down there.' Peter pointed through the large windows to paddocks on either side of the river some distance away.

The river stopped flowing during the drought that started in 1895 and lasted for seven years. Eighty million sheep died throughout the country during that time. Peter's predecessors had to drive their cattle to the mountains, where men with axes cut down she-oak trees so the animals could eat the leaves.

When the good seasons returned a big mob came through heading for the high country. The Sutherlands built their herd up from some of those cows.

'One of 'em,' Peter explained, 'had a perfect grey calf, a freak of nature.'

I asked Peter where he thought the Murray started. His story was the same as the other locals, but he did concede that some called the river that began where I had walked the Murray, while others said it was the Indi. 'Aboriginals reckon it's where the Indi meets the Swampy Plains.'

Walking through the front paddock, Peter pointed out the boundary of his property, the backwater of the Hume Dam that was created in 1956 and which used '56 000 acres of the best country you'll ever see in the world'.

'When I came here all the flats were covered with silver tussock,' Peter said wistfully. 'In some places it'd grown over like a big dome and the cattle hid in there and you'd spend days on horseback trying to find 'em.' Now, when the dam levels are high, some of Peter's paddocks are 'pretty bloody useless'.

The dam was '242 miles around, same distance as from here to Melbourne,' Peter explained, 'and shallow when we need depth; that's why we lose so much water.'

We leant on the fence and Peter pointed to the site where the original homestead was built in 1845 before his family arrived. A tribe of Aborigines had once surrounded the settlers so they couldn't get out. The locals waited patiently and eventually the settlers had to make a run for it, but they were all speared to death and the homestead burnt down.

'They were found quite a few days later and were all buried in one grave,' Peter said. 'When my mob arrived there was a hoodoo on the place and the blackfellas wouldn't come back.'

The family rebuilt the homestead out of stone on the riverbank with little fortress holes in the walls, one big room with beds at one end and a living area at the other. The huge clumps of rushes that had concealed the attackers were removed.

Peter and I drove down to the river and he showed me the grave. There was a bit of the stone left lying around but not much else. The settlers must have been terrified, surrounded with not much chance of escape. And the Aborigines, too, would have been fearing for their future after the invasion of their land.

So what did the river mean to Peter?

'Family,' he answered eventually. 'We wouldn't be here without the river. Without it there's no life. It's a creature. The Aborigines loved this place, it was their life and they never ventured far away from it. Now it's the same for us.'

I had wanted to make Tallangatta that night but instead decided to camp in the public reserve on the banks of the Hume Dam. In the morning the sun threw shadows across the water from the hundreds of dead trees that had been drowned; sacrificed when the water covered them. Beautiful red and blue birds joined me, along with a few magpies warbling in the new day.

Tallangatta calls itself 'The Town that Moved' with good reason. It was in the way of 'progress' when the dam was built, so they shifted it. Well, shifted most of it. The brick buildings were demolished, and only some of those built from wood were moved.

In 1918 the River Murray Commission decided it needed a dam to provide reliable irrigation water for farmers downstream. Actually, it needed a number of dams along the length of the river—but it wasn't a bad idea, really. Instead of the winter water flowing away, the plan was to store it in lakes and then send it downstream in summer to meet the demands of irrigators. About twenty-five times the volume of water in Sydney Harbour is taken out of the Murray each year, 95 per cent going to irrigation.

The first section of the Hume Reservoir—or Hume Dam—was completed in 1936, and expanded in 1956 when the 'New Tallangatta' township was officially opened. When the really dry periods arrive the water level drops and you can see the site of the old town, including the main street, the embankment of the old railway and the roads in and out of the town.

It was hard to imagine the river before the dam was in place. And with all that water on top of it, was the river still there? Were there canyons on the floor of the dam where the river still flowed? And how unbecoming it was for the river. Flowing into the sea was the end of a journey, it had meaning, but disappearing into the anonymity of a huge man-made dam was not the way it should be. Still, it would emerge in some fashion on the other side. For that, at least, I was grateful.

Mid-autumn

Hume Dam to Yarrawonga

The cool of autumn in the Upper Murray was mellowed by the warmth of the colours. Deciduous European trees dotted through the hillsides had changed their appearance considerably since my last visit. Leaves of varying colours were strewn across the ground, though some trees clung obstinately to the last of them. Around the Hume Dam, willows had begun depositing their yellow and brown clothes in the waters, no doubt causing Betty Walton of Tintaldra more of her annual concern. My appearance had changed also. The last visit was made wearing shorts and T-shirts, but now jumpers and jeans had been added to the bag.

Even though the boat had been towed back to try to make at least part of the voyage on water, I decided not to take it out on the dam. Riding around out there had no point. Anyway, the water level was very low, down to under 20 per cent capacity, so all that I wanted to see—which wasn't much—could be seen from the bank.

On the outlet side of the dam wall, water leaked down the concrete slipway and into the river, now much wider than it had been when entering the dam. The river had found its way again, although its fresh, youthful exuberance had disappeared. The clear, clean water had gone and it was now a brownish colour, and it would stay that way for the rest of its journey.

The Hume Dam was hailed as one of the great Australian engineering feats. One of the first large-scale intergovernmental projects facilitated by Federation, the construction employed a thousand men; nine of them would lose their lives. Horses and steam engines were the main source of mechanical assistance, along with plenty of hard manual labour. The dam's basic function was to make sure the Murray never again stopped flowing, as it did in the drought years of 1914 and 1915.

Originally the dam was completed in 1936, but between 1950 and 1961 further work increased its capacity. Holding four times more water than Sydney Harbour, it was slightly smaller than the Dartmouth Dam built on the Mitta Mitta River, which also supplemented flows into the Murray.

Standing on the dam wall reminded me of the Snowy Mountains Scheme. The scheme changed the course of the Snowy and the Murray rivers, diverting their water for irrigation 'to feed a growing nation', and to supply electricity for homes and industries. It took twenty-five years to complete and over one hundred thousand people from all over the world took part, many of whom began their new lives in the Bonegilla Migrant Reception and Training Centre.

Said to be the first cattle station in Victoria, Bonegilla had various meanings in the local Aboriginal language, including 'big waterhole', 'deep water' and 'big cattle camp'. Part of the run was divided up in the late 1800s and in 1946 an ex-army camp in the area that kept the original name, a couple of kilometres away from the dam, became a refuge for people who had had their lives thrown into chaos by World War II. Bonegilla was a place where people arrived, in many cases, with nothing but dreams. Around 320 000 people from over thirty-five ethnic groups passed through. It later became what was supposed to be temporary accommodation for migrants who had been offered free or assisted passage in return for two years of labouring for the government. When they'd completed their obligations, the migrants were free to go anywhere.

It only took a few minutes to reach Bonegilla from the Hume Dam. There was not much to see apart from a few of the huts which formed the main part of a half-finished project designed to become a cultural heritage site. After walking around the huts I sat for a minute on one of the wooden steps leading into a corrugated-iron building that boasted one window per room.

My mind travelled back to a place close to where we had lived in England—the Friday Bridge Refugee Camp, set up after World War II. On occasion, my mother and father, together with some of their friends, spent time entertaining the occupants. Some of the refugees would visit our home. One was a gigantic black man who smoked cigarettes that filled the house with the exotic smells of faraway lands. He wore a coloured hat that fitted his huge head perfectly and a great big shawl that was thick and heavy. To me he was 'the man in the blanket'. I wondered if he knew anyone that had come to Bonegilla.

The Bonegilla Migrant Experience, a museum some 10 kilometres away in Albury, offered much more. Near the entrance a circular mosaic was inlaid with quotes from those who had experienced the camp.

'It was a different world' was one that struck me. Another spoke of spending the warm nights listening to Radio Roma. Others were of how local families invited them into their homes and how mothers held their families together, while perhaps the most poignant mentioned their happiness with freedom.

Inside the museum, after studying the exhibits in the Aboriginal section and the Chinese area, I came across an old man and his granddaughter as they stood peering at a photograph. He introduced himself as Frank, but admitted his real name was Franz. His granddaughter was Tracey.

'Fair-dinkum name, eh?' asked Frank, laughing.

He'd brought Tracey to the museum to show her something of her heritage, to show her the place where he'd arrived before Christmas 1950 to work on the Snowy Scheme. It was only a labouring job and, Frank said, it was very hard work. He shrugged his shoulders. 'That's how it was, we did what we had to do.' After pausing for a moment Frank continued. 'It felt good, changing nature, you know?'

It wasn't until a few years later that Frank realised that although life was pretty good for the men, it was much harder for the women. But at night in the huts when they were together with their families and friends, they'd sing and dance and nothing else mattered. They'd talk about their new home and about how they liked Australia.

Many of Frank's friends left Bonegilla to live in the cities, but others settled in river towns. Frank remembered the hot summer evenings when they would walk down to the Murray and swim. 'Ah, the river,' he sighed. 'We catch yabbies, we swam, we changed it a bit and now everyone else change it a lot.'

Before they left Frank showed Tracey a picture of the ship that brought him to Australia, then held her hand as they crossed the busy street at the lights.

Albury was the start of what was known as the Riverine Plains, a flat expanse of the country that continued past Swan Hill. This was where the Wiradjuri people knew the river as Millewa. It was also where Hamilton Hume and William Hovell had discovered the Murray in 1824. Hovell named the river the Hume—'he being the first that saw it'. Little did he know then that, despite his gesture, Hume had already decided to name the river after his father Andrew, a superintendent of convicts in Sydney.

On their journey from Sydney to Port Phillip, Hume and Hovell had come across, 'a beautiful stream, not less than eighty yards in breadth and of considerable depth' just along from where the museum now stood. The river was too broad to ford there so the men explored further upstream and found a suitable place a short distance away. I was able to see for myself evidence of the men's visit. Near the river, in what was called naturally enough, Hovell Tree Park, was a tree that Hovell marked with his initials on 17 November 1824. (The explorers' journals record the date as actually being the sixteenth, and Hovell recarved the correct figures on a later visit.) Bark had long since grown over Hovell's markings, while another tree, marked by Hume a short distance away, was destroyed by fire in the 1840s.

A few years later, Major Thomas Mitchell crossed just downstream from where the city now stands. Originally known as The Crossing, it was where tens of thousands of sheep were driven across the river to the markets in Melbourne.

Apart from the cattle and sheep stations, the many German settlers from South Australia who moved to the district in the 1800s established a local wine industry. Most came by river, with one group taking almost two months on the journey. They were well accepted, even to the extent of the local paper regularly publishing one of its pages in German.

Although founded at a similar time, Albury is almost twice the size of Wodonga, the city on the Victorian side of the river. Although they are now the biggest cities along the river, neither town prospered until the 1850s gold rush brought thousands of miners to the area. Until then there were never more than sixty or so people living in the vicinity.

Squabbling between the two state governments didn't help. After Victoria separated from New South Wales, both colonies set up Tariff Stations for taxes to be paid when transporting goods across the border. When they were first established, tariffs were only fixed on items such as tobacco, wine and spirits, but soon they were placed on almost everything, including livestock. While this meant there were opportunities for lucrative government jobs—and for smugglers—there was a distinct disadvantage for farmers who wanted to sell their goods in Melbourne rather than Sydney.

An example of the absurd nature of tariffs was when someone from Albury who worked across the border would be charged for the tea and tobacco in their lunch box, then charged again if there was any left on the way home. Even workers on the bridge were required to pay duty on their tools.

The railway came to Wodonga from Melbourne in 1873 and from Sydney to Albury in 1881. Each colony had their own gauge and although the gap between the cities was just five kilometres it took another three years before they were linked. There were even arguments between the towns about the time. As New South Wales was the senior colony it was twenty-five minutes ahead of Victoria so, rather than make the time the same, two clocks were installed at the Albury station. As Federation grew closer, it was even proposed that Albury become the national capital as its access to rail, road and river transport would benefit everyone. In New South Wales, it was felt that Victoria was responsible for Canberra eventually winning out.

I'd planned to take the tinnie on an exploratory trip around Albury but the river was suffering. Standing close to the water's edge, it seemed as though I'd be hurting it even more if it had to indulge my motor when it was struggling to provide enough water to keep flowing.

My tinnie wasn't the only boat inconvenienced. At the nearby wharf the PS *Cumberoona* was listing to starboard at a significant angle, a victim of the low river. A sign near the gangway explained that she wouldn't be cruising the river for some time. The first *Cumberoona* had carried wool and passengers during the 1860s, but after moving to South Australia in 1887 she was snagged and sank. Refloated, she was repaired and finally went down after hitting rocks on the Darling two years later. This new *Cumberoona* wasn't a real paddle-steamer, simply a replica built to give tourists a taste of the river experience.

Even though one of the first steamers on the river was named after the town, Albury never had much of the riverboat trade thanks to the snags which made it barely navigable. Several attempts were made to overcome the snagging. To begin with logs would be cut off by axe when the river was low. When rivers were high this solved the problem but when the river dropped the logs were still there, waiting just under the surface.

Snagging teams were also prevalent at one time. A vessel named the *Grappler* had a huge crane that could lift up to 15 tonnes and employed South Sea Islanders to dive down and attach the chains and grapples to the logs that were to be shifted. (Later, men in diving suits would be used.) Ultimately, though, the job was too great and the rewards too little.

I'd read in E.J. Brady's book *River Rovers* about what he termed 'Hell's Gates'—some 30 kilometres, by river, from Albury—and wanted to see what he was talking about—maybe I could even make my way through them. After unintentionally driving through a few wrong gates, and being barked at by aggressive farm dogs, a track brought me close to where the Gates should have been. This was where the old course of the Murray had changed, one of the most challenging navigational tasks for river captains. Even though this might not have been the right place, the amount of half-hidden snags and recently fallen trees told me to leave the boat on the trailer. Brady had written eloquently about his problems and that was good enough for me.

> *The river yelled and boiled; snags snapped at us with malignant teeth. We hit once but the force of the current hurled us around. The boat completed a flying circle, leapt a submerged log and shot out into the broad water like a switch-back car. It was exhilarating work.*

I found a much more tranquil place a few kilometres further on the road to Howlong. The Wonga Wetlands used waste water from Albury in an attempt to return a portion of the river to its original state by bringing life back to an area that once flooded naturally. The river's natural flow had altered since the building of the Hume Dam; floodplains, wetlands and billabongs had dried out, destroying a natural bird and fish-breeding place.

Signs appeared everywhere in the grounds. 'Do Not Drink the Water'; 'Do Not Enter the Water'; 'Beware of Snakes'; 'Keep on the Walking Tracks'. The best one was 'No Animals' which, the sign added, included cats, dogs and horses—just in case the reader didn't know they were animals!

A note on the door of the office said that John and Mike weren't in, but if needed they could be reached on a mobile phone. I decided to keep going.

Half an hour later, in Howlong, I enjoyed the sun at what appeared to be the oldest shop in town. The tin roof was rusting in places and the signs attached to it needed repairs. One of the posts holding up the verandah was leaning towards the wall. The paint on everything was peeling. On a tin seat under the verandah, I sipped a coffee and devoured a tasty homemade muffin while studying the council workers at the crossroads.

There was not much traffic and what there was moved slowly, but there were still half a dozen men in the middle of the road. Two held signs to control the traffic flow, while the other four watched. I presumed the watchers would take over when the first pair became exhausted.

Everyone who walked past me nodded, smiled, or said hello. A couple of kids skating along the footpath pulled up, flipped their boards into their hands and asked what I was doing. When I countered by asking why they weren't at school, their reply was to drop their skateboards with a clatter and push themselves off along the pavement.

I tried the tinnie again in the river near the Howlong Lions Park, where the Black Swan anabranch heads off through the countryside before rejoining a few kilometres downstream. The shallow water meant the motor had to be lifted in some places to avoid the bottom, the propeller screaming a couple of times after being lifted too high. Travelling upstream for a short distance, I passed Parlour Creek and came to the bridge at the Black Swamp lagoon where sandbars on both banks had almost joined. With the bottom of the boat scraping some of the many snags protruding from the water, the only sensible thing was to head back.

The bloke who served me at the Howlong garage stated the obvious. That as well as being the curse of inland Australia, drought also harmed the river. Tall, bony and wearing overalls that had seen many greasy days, he didn't have anything new to say but he was certainly up for a chat.

As much as the Hume and Dartmouth Dams helped this part of the river, he went on as he checked the oil, it can't flow without rain during the winter. Everything that gave the Murray sustenance was now dry, or if not dry then certainly low and very slow. 'No rain, no flow, no water,' he said, slamming the bonnet down and wiping his hands.

I drove back to the lagoon, pitched my small tent on the sand and began reading Kath and Leon Bentley's *River of Islands* by gaslight. The couple had charted the river from the Hume Dam to Yarrawonga, and had been amazed by the number of islands they had come across.

The book told a story about the first overland mail run from Melbourne to Sydney, made by a John Bourke. After being wounded by a spear near the Ovens River, then accosted by a man with a gun, he tried to swim his horse across the river near Howlong, only for the animal to become stuck in the mud. Bourke then took off the saddlebags holding the mail and swam the river before setting off, naked, for the nearest station. Attacked by a pack of about fifty dogs he eventually found sanctuary in the branches of a huge red gum while the dogs howled around the base. The station owner soon appeared and, after scaring the dogs away with his gun, inquired as to the identity of this person in the tree. Bourke replied that he was 'Her Majesty's Mail from Melbourne.' The station owner laughed and said if that was the case then he didn't think much of his uniform.

Thinking about John Bourke and his troubles made me drowsy and, after turning off the gentle hiss of the gas lamp, the only sound came from the occasional car as it rumbled across the bridge.

The view when driving towards the famous Rutherglen wine district is one of almost continuous vineyard. The town itself is some nine kilometres from the river but the sixteen or so wineries in the district use its water to help create some of the country's finest wines. All Saints winery near Wahgunyah, a small town on the Victorian side of the river from Corowa, was my first stop.

Wahgunyah is thought to be the local Aboriginal word for 'big camp' and was where John Foord took up a pastoral run in 1841, the first in the district. He established a punt across the river in 1857 and soon after paddle-steamers took passengers and goods to Echuca for connection to the railway. Foord was also one of the first to think about irrigation. Indeed, by 1860 he had proposed three schemes, the first a month after he had arrived. But they were all considered too costly.

Known as Chinatown early in its existence for the hundreds of Chinese who settled there for the gold rush, Wahgunyah once had a joss house and two burning towers used for Chinese funerals. In a different religious slant, it also had the 'Mass Tree', marking the place where the first mass in the district was held near Sunday Creek.

All Saints winery—now owned by the Brown family—was founded in 1864 by a couple of enterprising Scotsmen, George Sutherland Smith and John Banks, who decided that their winery would be a castle based on their memory of the Castle of Mey in Caithness. Two rows of stately 120-year-old elm trees, halfway through losing their leaves, lined the driveway. These, together with the vines, typified autumn, an explosion of browns, reds and vermilions.

Inside the main building, Eliza Brown, marketing manager of the family business, admitted to being sad when the river was dry. 'When it's like this, life around here is different. We change, the river changes, and it's then we understand how everything we do is affected by it and everything we do affects it.' She described the river as being like a 'big fat man with a girth problem', getting wider all the time. The water was rising and dropping so much, trees were falling in and the banks were eroding. 'He's getting fatter and thinner almost at the same time, and no one's helping him. We want to look after it; we need to look after it,' she said shrugging her shoulders. 'After all, if we don't, what happens?'

Although the Rutherglen district had nearly twenty wineries nearby all pumping water from the Murray, Eliza had told me that vineyards weren't a real problem for the river, as unlike other farms they didn't need much water. In fact, the vines needed a bit of hardship to produce their best fruit, so the owners are as frugal with water as they can be.

Eliza was summoned to take some visiting wine buyers around but left me to walk through the great hall and see the eighty-year-old wine barrels containing wines of similar vintage. On a nearby wall was a plaque for Australia's first wine gold medal, awarded in London in 1873—a victory in which the Murray must have shared. I checked out the castle walls and the restaurant and was intrigued by the corrugated-iron building known as the Chinese Dormitory. A hundred years old and the only one of its type, this was where Chinese prospectors were billeted when they came to work at the vineyard after the gold rush petered out at nearby Beechworth. They worked in the vineyards in sweltering heat during the day and then tried to sleep in an iron dormitory.

I crossed the river back to Corowa on the John Foord Bridge, one of just thirty-two road and five railway bridges spanning the river. Corowa was founded during the 1850s as the result of the surge in riverboat traffic and its proximity to the Beech-worth gold mines. In the local Aboriginal language, Corowa means 'rocky river', a reference to rocks across the river nearby. The name could also derive from 'currawa', referring to the Murray Pine from which the Aborigines retrieved gum for their spears.

The town claims to be the birthplace of Federation. Prior to 1901 Australia consisted of six separate colonies each governed by its own parliaments, which—as I learnt in Albury—caused confusion and frustration when dealing with customs and tariffs, mainly on the river border. This dislike of custom duties between New South Wales and Victoria was the main motiva-tion behind Corowa hosting the 1893 Federation Conference. Organised by the Local Border Federation League, the confer-ence was held in the Corowa Court House with representatives from Federation Leagues, the Australian Natives Association, trading and commercial bodies, and parliamentarians from New South Wales and Victoria. At the conference, a motion which was to change both the direction and pace of Federa-tion was carried unanimously. It called for each of the Colonial Parliaments to appoint representatives to attend a convention that would ultimately establish a Federal Constitution for Australia. In his speech to the assembled delegates, the Victorian Premier, a certain Mr Patterson, said: 'When a man who comes here from Victoria is regarded as a foreigner and a woman who goes to Wahgunyah is treated as a smuggler, liable to be stuck by police and customs, it is time some change was made.'

The town certainly has some magnificent buildings from that period. One of which—the Federation Museum—was locked and bolted. A notice on the door said that it was only open on weekends or selected holidays. In the main street, away from all the grandiose reflections of the past, stood a wide-verandahed building with a huge metal sign above it reading 'REX'. A giant arrow pointing towards the footpath would once have proudly blinked in neon but was now quietly rusting away. The old cinema, long since gone, had become a discount clothes and junk shop.

At the caravan park the river was just a trickle of water between two rows of sand. There was no chance of a boat trip. The woman in the office was unhappy. She couldn't remember the river ever being so bad.

'Generally the rains have helped keep it up a bit, but without them no one wants to come here,' she lamented. 'Have a look around—I know it's autumn but we're still pretty quiet.'

The river height—or lack of it—showed off the sandbars. Perfect white sand on either side that stretched away in the distance like beaches, although I suspected there wouldn't have been the syringes and other rubbish found at Bondi or St Kilda.

Sitting at a large wooden table outside his caravan, which was parked in the last row before the riverbank—or at least where the river and the bank would normally have met—an older man wearing a striped woollen beanie was reading a paper. He looked up as I approached, folded his paper and then his arms. Jack had been regularly coming up at this time of year, to 'spend a few months away from Melbourne and enjoy some quiet time'. It was never quite as warm but he didn't like the crowds of summer. He hated to see the river suffer.

'What can we do to help it?' he asked as he looked at the fallen trees exposed by the water level. 'Sounds stupid prob'ly, but I think I can hear it groaning at times.'

Further along the river and a short distance inland from the caravan park was the Corowa-Rutherglen football ground.

A good torpedo punt from the wing would land the ball in the water. At the entrance an old tree had been carved into a huge Australian Rules pack with a wooden figure rising sublimely from the top of a clutch of bodies, his hands grasping the football. No matter whether the team was successful or not, the carving would remind those who entered the ground of the promise of hope, of the return to good times.

I launched the boat again a few kilometres out of town at Snake Island, wanting to find out how big the island was and whether indeed there were any snakes. The voyage didn't last long, however, as the motor wouldn't start. I pulled and pulled and pleaded and cursed and stamped my feet, none of which worked. Deflated and frustrated, not to mention sore-shouldered, I hauled it out again, at the same time slipping in the mud. Finding yourself face down in shallow, muddy, cold water is not good for one's disposition so I sat on the bank, discarded my sodden shoes and jeans, and prepared to start again. It took a few minutes to gather myself.

I'd been trying to establish a more personal connection with the river. I'd talked to it, even played music for it, but maybe I was being too familiar. Perhaps this was the Murray's way of reminding me not to take it for granted. The second attempt to load the boat was more successful.

After pitching the tent a little way from the bank, and looking forward to an evening of solitude, an ordinary-looking black and white farm dog wandered up. It must have gone for a walk or fallen off a ute. It wouldn't come close but sat, then lay down and watched me. Once the fire was lit, and after I'd ignored it for a few minutes, it ventured closer and sat opposite me. He watched hungrily as I opened a tin of beans and cooked toast in the coals, then eagerly devoured the few crusts chucked his way. During our feast I asked him if he knew anything about boat motors but he just kept staring at me, mouth open, tongue out. He didn't respond, either, to questions about his feelings for the river; whether he jumped in it regularly, whether his owner was angry when he did, or if he had swum any sheep through it.

He must have been a long way from home. There were no lights indicating a house anywhere along the bank. Even from the higher ground on the road, there were no signs of life.

The dog cocked his head to one side and seemed interested in me stretching a rope carefully near the fire on which to hang my wet clothes. Inside the tent the glow of the fire marked a canine shadow on the thin canvas.

My companion must have stayed the night, as he barked a couple of times at some rustling in the bushes, but in the morning there was no sign of him. Disappointed, I walked up and down, and called and whistled, but he'd vanished.

The problem with the outboard motor, even with my severely limited mechanical ability, was easily solved. The petrol tank was at an angle too severe for the pick-up tube to find the fuel. With an engine that would now start, I put the boat in close to where the Ovens River joined the Murray, near the start of Lake Mulwala. The Ovens was low as well but I wasn't interested in exploring. That was not my river.

Lake Mulwala was formed when the Yarrawonga Weir was built. The biggest of the thirteen weirs on the river, Yarrawonga didn't have a lock so the only way to move up or downstream was to take boats out. When the lake was being created it was suggested the trees from the area should be cleared. Men with saws and axes spent years felling huge gums but didn't get far upstream. And many of those trees they did cut down were left where they fell so when the lake is drained the look of the mass of tangled wood that is always just below the surface makes the lake's waterskiers a touch uncomfortable.

At the top end of the lake, near the Ovens River junction, dead trees abounded; branches at different angles, all tortured, all leafless, all drowned. Red gums need to be flooded every so often, but when it occurs constantly they die.

There was an eerie feeling among the trees. Quiet and cool and morose; a timber graveyard and the river was the keeper, looking after the ghosts.

The boating exercise needed slow and careful navigation to keep clear of the red markers that indicated shallow water. A sign said it was 2024 kilometres to the Murray mouth.

A few other boats were searching for fish and at one tree a cheery and obviously experienced fisherman helped me tie up. He was after a cod but wasn't having much luck. 'Come out here where it's quiet,' he said, 'not heaps of tourists, and there's always supposed to be the chance of a fish.'

He noticed I had no rod and, grinning, told me that there wasn't much chance of getting anything without one. I replied that rods and me and cod were fairly useless together. After an hour or so of idle chat, he reeled in his line and announced that he was going back to Yarrawonga, using part of the song—'I'm going back again to Yarrawonga'—as his exit line.

The song was written during World War I. Neil McBeath was chief draughtsman for General Monash in France. One day, as they were planning another attack, they heard one relieving soldier call out to the wounded being brought back from the front line on stretchers how lucky they were to be going back to Australia. One of the wounded raised himself from his stretcher and said, 'Not on your life, mate. I'm going back again to Yarrawonga.' When he returned after the war, McBeath penned the song.

I'm going back again to Yarrawonga,
In Yarrawonga, I'll linger longer.
I'm going back again to Yarrawonga,
To the land of the kangaroo.

Hamilton Hume established the first station in the area when he took up land for his sister-in-law Elizabeth, whose husband had been shot by a bushranger, leaving her with nine children to support. The land included 20 kilometres of river frontage and was called Yarroweyah, which later was changed to Yarrawonga.

Much of the district's history was housed in a big tin shed —the Pioneer Museum. Devoid of visitors, it was about to close for the day when Ian Douglas, vice-president of the local historical society, welcomed me.

The son of a farmer, Ian had lived on the river for most of his seventy years, and had an encyclopaedic knowledge of all things Yarrawongan. Apart from school, his boyhood was spent fishing, hunting, and catching crayfish. When the river flooded, he and his brother would put a wire across the river downstream to collect all the boats that would be carried away with the river's surge. 'We'd get five bob for each one we rescued,' Ian said, 'and we'd row 'em back to the owners.'

Levee banks have now made a difference, but in those days floods would come right up to their door on the farm. 'One year, I remember them catching an eight-pound cod on the football oval; that'll never happen again.'

Ian once caught an 89-pound cod and it 'just fitted across the back seat of me Dodge Four car.'

He reckoned the river was still pretty good around Yarrawonga although he conceded that it was 'a bit buggered down further'.

I headed for the weir, stopping briefly at the Yarrawonga Bridge to look at the old customs house, a tiny weatherboard building where authorities had collected the much-despised taxes from those taking goods across the river. A sign dating back to 1894 announced that 'all persons having goods in their possession and about to enter the colony of New South Wales must first report to the customs house'. Peering through the sole window I could make out a small wooden table and chair sitting in one corner. An ancient kerosene lamp sat on the table next to a pen and ink stand.

You can drive across the weir at Yarrawonga, or walk or jog across it, which many do. You can also sit in the small park and watch the water trickle through the gates. I sat in the park near a large rock which had a couple of plaques attached. One told the story of the 'inter-governmental conference on the waters of the River Murray at Corowa in 1902'. This conference

gave rise to one of the great engineering initiatives of the new Federation—the creation of the River Murray Commission in 1915 by the governments of New South Wales, Victoria, South Australia and The Federal, to provide equitable and efficient and sustainable use of the waters of the River Murray.

The aim of the Commission was to build a series of locks and weirs from Yarrawonga to the mouth which would control the water and help with flooding, irrigation and the like. The lake behind the weir was full, which was just as well as two huge channels—the Mulwala channel to New South Wales and the Yarrawonga channel to Victoria—took vast amounts of water to the dry farming land.

Although there was no lock for boats to move beyond the weir there were two other items of interest. One was the hydro-electric power station which contributed to the electricity of the state; the other was a new 'fishway', designed to allow fish passage into Lake Mulwala.

When fish came up river they would be attracted to the entrance by what was termed an 'attractant flow'. They would then make their way, theoretically at least, through different chambers before swimming into the lake. A 'separation cage' in the fishway to catch the dreaded European carp was based on the fact that carp tend to jump when enclosed and native fish don't. So when carp swim into the fishway they jump over a wall into the cage and are then removed. The largest project of its kind in the world, the fishways would provide fish with continuous passage, if they so desired, the complete length of the Murray. This was the third fishway that was under construction, with the rest expected to be in place in the next couple of years. Workmen repairing parts of the weir were not overly confident that the fishway worked. One told me his mate had seen blokes collecting fish in crates and releasing them in the lake.

After booking in at Burke's Royal Mail Hotel/Motel for the night I headed to the bar for a beer and became caught in the middle of an argument about football tipping. Leaving the protagonists to their very colourful discussion, I walked over to the window where Bert, an older regular who had heard it all before, was staring aimlessly into the street while rolling a smoke. He looked up, quickly informing me that although he had lived in Yarrawonga all his life he didn't feel much like talking. Instead, he advised me to head across the street to talk to the hairdresser, Dennis 'Tippy' Lean, the president of Yarrawonga Fishing Club.

Tippy's family had been taking care of men's hair in the same shop since his grandfather started the business. 'He trained Dad and Dad trained me.' Tippy's sons, however, were not interested in carrying on the family tradition so the future was bleak for this old-fashioned barber shop.

On a shelf next to a large mirror in front of the single barber's chair was a collection of old tobacco tins—Log Cabin, Champion, Mick McQuade Cut—plus boxes of Redheads matches of varying age. Posters of fish and waterfowl were stuck on the wall while an old cabinet held fishing reels of all ages, shapes and sizes, for as much as Tippy was a barber, he was also a fishing gear retailer, and throughout the shop were rods, knives, lures and other fishing paraphernalia.

Tippy remembered that when he was a young bloke there were only about twelve wooden rowing boats in a town with a population of a couple of thousand. 'That was before the weir came. Now we have four thousand people or so and every house has got a boat, knows someone who's got a boat or knows someone that brings a boat up here.' All boats were a problem to some extent, he said, with their wake washing away the bank and their owners catching the diminishing supplies of fish.

The last customer of the day sat down in the chair and, in between snips, Tippy recalled his father's story of how sometimes, after school, he would be sent to catch a cod for tea. Tippy's dad would head off to where the weir is now, taking his long bamboo rod with a bit of line and a spinner on it, drag it back and forth, catch a cod and take it home to his mother.

As a kid, Tippy would row his specially made tin boat around the lake before school, trying to catch a fish, then when the lake was emptied so that repairs could be carried out on the weir gates, he and his mates would nail old shoes to slats of wood and 'ski' across the mudflats.

The haircut was finished quickly as the customer was almost bald, and after he bought a packet of tobacco and papers the two of them told me stories about fishing near the golf course and catching cod with golf balls in their stomachs. Tippy's best was three but he had a mate whose record was five, while the newly shorn customer had caught one that had swallowed a full can of beer. 'Cod'll eat anything when they're on the bite.'

'It's my life, really, the river,' Tippy admitted. 'It might sound wacky but it feels like I own it, it's always been there for me.' He said he became very aggressive when people told him the river was dying. 'I don't know how they can say that. I know there's a few problems but around here it's as good as I can remember.'

'How often do you fish?' I asked before leaving.

'Not as often as I'd like,' he grinned, 'but I've heard the redfin are on the bite; reckon I'll go tomorrow and try and get a feed, that's if I don't get a bloody carp.'

European carp were introduced to Lake Hawthorn near Mildura in the early 1970s for aquaculture, but the fish escaped during a flood and since then have become a menace along the length of the Murray, especially in South Australia. Dwelling on the bottom of the river, carp suck up everything like scaly vacuum cleaners and blow out what they don't like. They don't mind salinity and couldn't care less about pollution, so as the river becomes more dirty the carp thrive. They also contribute to erosion of the banks by undermining them on their sucking explorations.

There is some hope, though. Exports have begun to Europe, where they are made into sausages, fish fingers and steaks as well as sushi and smoked carp pâté. Tippy reckoned the Europeans were welcome to them. 'The Murray has a never-ending supply of the stinking things.'

Redfin, although regarded by some fishermen as a pest because they eat the native fish, also have their good points. When European carp arrived they destroyed the habitat in which the redfin bred. That, in turn, allowed the native fish to breed again and they began to eat the small carp. Although it has taken a long while, the balance has started to return and now Murray cod are plentiful, especially in the middle reaches of the river.

The pub was quiet when I returned. Bert had left, the tipsters had gone home, the bar was almost empty. The double bed in my room, while not quite as romantic as a night under the stars, was nevertheless more than acceptable for a tired, aching body that had endured six nights in a cramped swag and tent.

In the morning I walked along the lake front, watching swans glide past and other walkers enjoying the atmosphere of the sun rising in our eyes. A number of the houses had private jetties under the willow trees—small, square floating pontoons. A couple of the jetties had outdoor settings on them while one had a canvas cover in case the sun became too hot. Early morning fishermen tried their luck from the bank and a number of boats headed towards the dead trees, the sun flashing from their metal sides.

On the way back, I saw Tippy sweeping the footpath. 'Good day for it,' he yelled across the street. He was right, but it was time for me to head home.

Early Winter

Yarrawonga to Picnic Point

The rains had arrived by the time I returned to the river in early winter. Myriad creeks and drains and tributaries had gathered the liquid offerings from two states and given it to the Murray. Like a runner taking a cup from the benches during a marathon, the river had needed a drink, and while it wasn't back to peak condition it had at least been freshened. The drink wouldn't last long but would keep it going for a while.

The caravan park below the weir at Yarrawonga is the traditional starting place for the world's longest canoe race, the Murray Marathon, in which paddlers in all sorts of craft make their way to Swan Hill over a five-day period that finishes each New Year's Eve. The marathon began in 1969 when ten friends paddled their way down the river, raising $250 for the Red Cross. Now there are around 800 competitors who raise around $300 000.

Entrants gather at the park and are awakened at dawn on the opening day to the sounds of 'Morning Has Broken' blaring through loudspeakers mounted on the roof of a car. They are sent on their way when a century-old blunderbuss explodes the morning air. Each day the same ritual occurs. Each day the ritual commences a bit later.

I'd followed the marathon one year—not as a contestant, but to follow and support a couple of younger people who battled everything the river, nature and their minds could throw up. Athough never quite courageous enough to enter the race I was, after due consideration, determined to test myself in a similar vein. I decided to paddle from Yarrawonga to Picnic Point, a distance of almost 200 kilometres. I wanted to know the river more intimately, to try to fully understand what it meant to me, to see whether it was ready to communicate. We had some things to discuss, and for that the river and I needed to be alone.

My craft was a Canadian canoe, which, although not the fastest, was a vessel with plenty of space for gear and, importantly, would more than likely stay upright.

Competitors in the marathon said that backs and backsides were their biggest problems, as were blisters on hands and aching wrists and shoulders—not to mention the heat of summer. All of this was of no concern to me, since this was winter and I wasn't racing, just out for what I hoped would be a leisurely five-day paddle. Only a couple of hours in the morning then a couple more in the afternoon, at least double the time they would take. Besides, in my kit of necessities there was a pair of gloves to protect my hands and a pillow for my backside. Around my waist was a brace to keep my back from falling apart while a large hat and a pair of sunglasses would protect me from whatever sun was going to appear. Added to this was a collection of insect repellants, creams and pills.

Under an angry winter sky and laden with tent and swag in the bow, I stroked the canoe away from the bank. I could almost hear the river laughing as the craft wobbled uncontrollably for 20 metres or so. Remaining upright I called out as though it could hear me, 'See, I'm okay!'

Then the wobbling started again. It might have been a warning.

With new water and increased height, the current was quite swift and I quickly found a rhythm. As long as the canoe was guided rather than forced along, paddling was reasonably easy. I was confident it would stay that way. After all, in the marathon there were blokes a lot older than me who paddled a lot further. Ted Jackson, for instance. He was nearing his eightieth birthday and had completed eighteen marathons. Ted loved the challenge and had told me he did it to keep in shape. He held the record for the longest canoe trip in Australia. In his mid-sixties he'd paddled over 5000 kilometres in seventy-eight days from the Condamine River in Queensland to the mouth of the Murray. And fifteen years before that he canoed 4800 kilometres down the Mississippi with his son Norm. Another was seventy-eight-year-old Bill Scott, who used a canoe similar to mine and looked like a Red Indian in a Davy Crockett movie— up on one knee and sweeping the water behind him with a single paddle. Not a pleasant way to travel over 300 kilometres but Bill was a determined fellow.

Those men were on friendly terms with most rivers whereas mine was still getting to know me.

An hour later, the sky broke.

There is something distinctive and appealing about a river and the rain, although not when you're alone in a canoe and it is pouring. Not when you have another two or three hours of paddling before you can get out if it. And certainly not when it is dripping down your neck because the hat that was supposed to protect you from the sun did not do the same with the rain.

The cloudburst didn't last long, and although the rain persisted it was only light. As a precaution I tied up to a snag and made sure everything was covered and waterproof. After resuming my metronomic paddling I began to find the rain's noticeably symmetrical pattern on the surface of the river was hypnotic, although it didn't put off the welcome swallows. Named because they would fly around as though 'welcoming' paddle-steamers whenever they arrived in a town, they now splashed and flapped and dived around the canoe, their attention on a lone soul adrift in the weather.

Apart from many different birds, the first signs of life came after an hour when a caravan came into view. The blue and white marker on a nearby gum tree, combined with the maps from my charts, told me I had travelled about 24 kilometres and was at Nevin's East Beach. Who Nevin was and why it was his beach was a mystery, but the occupant of the caravan was George, a ruddy-faced chap with short and largely disappearing red hair. The rain had stopped and George was bent over a fire, trying to re-establish the flames by burning the daily paper sheet by sheet. Every time the flames got too close he'd let go, the paper would blow away and he'd chase it and stamp it into the sand. He eventually gave up. 'Stuff it,' he exclaimed as I approached. 'I'll do it when there's no wind.'

From a small place on the New South Wales coast George had been travelling around the country for over four years, stopping wherever something appealed to him. He decided he liked the Murray and had spent five weeks on the sandbar but, surprisingly, had no inclination to fish, nor did he own a boat.

'So what do you do?' I asked.

'Just sit around,' he replied. 'But I knit, and make tin men from old beer cans.' George explained that he knitted jumpers and scarves for friends and family, and also sold a few at local markets. He didn't explain the tin men.

George offered me a coffee that was as cold as the fire we sat beside. We didn't talk a great deal, although he did venture to say that he wasn't by himself. His wife, although inconspicuous, was with him. He asked me what I was doing.

'Geez!' He sounded surprised as I described my journey then stood up to depart.

George's wife appeared as he was pushing me gently out on the water.

'He's goin' down the river,' he told her as she joined him.

'Is he?' she asked.

'Yeah,' replied George. 'He is.'

The stop had done me the world of good. I had stretched my legs, released the tension in my back and given some much-needed relief to my knees. Back in the canoe my joints were all taking their time to become used to their limited space again. As I floated along the straights and drifted around the bends, blue and white markers appeared regularly on trees. In the 1990s the New South Wales Waterways and the South Australian Tourism Authority had placed markers on trees every two kilometres.

A man named Pearce conducted the original survey by rowing along the river, measuring, by link and chain, the distance in miles between Albury and Wentworth. He carved the figures into trees for the riverboat captains. Some of those trees still exist.

Victoria hadn't taken any part in the exercise, probably because the river was owned by the other two states. The Murray River is in New South Wales; the state border is the high water mark on the Victorian side. At one time the Murrumbidgee River was to be the border but apparently the surveying officer found 'Murrumbidgee' too hard to spell.

As the Murray changes course over the years, and billabongs, anabranches and lagoons continue to be created, it can be difficult to determine where the main watercourse is. In 1975 Maureen Wright, together with her husband Barry, renewed the old survey, charting the river from Renmark to Yarrawonga, and have updated their own charts seven times since that first effort. I made sure their book—*Murray River Charts*—was always close at hand.

The chart relating to my current position named it as Dufty's No 2 Beach, which would be followed by Bourke Beach, then Cobrawonga Beach, which was close to Killer Point and just downstream from Dead River Beach. These were but some of the one hundred beaches—or sandbars—along the river from Yarrawonga to Tocumwal, now some 70 kilometres away. They were all long expanses of pure sand, shiny, white and soft, all left from when the area was the sea.

Studying the charts and relating names to the beaches made the time pass and soon enough I was in sight of Horseshoe Bend. The river swept away from view as a marker attached to a stately tree informed me it was 1918 kilometres to the mouth. There, a sandbar that must have been 200 metres long stretched around the bend in front of the Barooga State Forest.

Exhausted from exertion unknown to my body for years, I slid the canoe onto the sand. After pitching the tent on firmer ground I built a fire with wood that was damp on the outside but which burned freely once warmed up. A large log served as a seat. Even though it was cold and wet it wasn't raining, but the sky was ominous. No stars would be seen that night.

The journey to Cobram early the next morning was uneventful. The sky had cleared somewhat but it appeared more rain could fall at any moment. The river looked elegant, cloaked in the grey of the day. As this powerful, reassuring force moved me along slowly, I studied what no artist could capture with a brush, what no photographer, no matter their lens or filter, could evoke: the smell of the air, the taste of the rain, the movement of the swirls, the eddies, the cutaways on the bends. The water formed a distinct V shape as it poured around a snag sticking out like Arthur's Excalibur while a bored shag removed its head from under a grey wing and looked at me briefly before returning to its own business.

Two hours later, with a refreshed soul—and after a drenching from a sudden cloudburst—the houseboat moorings at Cobram appeared.

Thompson's Beach is the largest and most well known of all the beaches on the river. Workmen on the new bridge said they'd keep an eye on the canoe during their lunch break so I walked the two kilometres into town. The shopping centre was built in a triangle with no obvious main street. The streets were quite empty although it would be different when the warmer weather arrived. In winter Thompson's Beach was barren, but in summer it was as 'busy as bloody Bondi', according to the woman in the café who served me a salad sandwich and asked in a rough voice, 'Ya want a bag or a plate, darl?'

'Plate, if that's okay,' I replied.

'Goodonya, darl,' were her parting words as she gave me change and left to serve the next in the queue of four, all of whom were staring at me. They could hardly be blamed—an unshaven, dirtily dressed, middle-aged man who wore a misshapen hat soaked by rain and who squelched quietly as he walked was probably not the most common winter sight in town.

After the others left the woman came to clear the table. She nodded towards me. 'How'd ya get like that, darl?'

'Just being a silly man.'

She grinned as she walked off. 'There's a few of youse about.'

In the paper shop, the enthusiastic man behind the counter told me how the river helped the district. 'Peaches, strawberries, a bit of broadacre stuff, plenty of dairy cows, we've got bloody everything.'

I stuck the newspaper in my coat pocket and only glanced at it upon returning to the beach. It was full of pictures and stories from London following the terrorist attacks on the underground. The paper was deposited in the nearest rubbish bin.

Yet even here world events were of particular concern. A man waiting with me at the counter in the paper shop had told me about Cobram's new population of escapees from the regime of Saddam Hussein. Almost four hundred Iraqis now lived in the town and at times they had some troubles; September 11 in 2001 was one instance. Then, a couple of years later, an Iraqi grocery store was burnt down. Things were slowly improving, said the man, but there was still a long way to go.

We talked about the other migrants to the area, such as the Italians and the Greeks.

'Yeah,' he said, 'it was easier for them; we went to the same church and drank at the same pub. They played footy, too.'

Despite the willingness of most people to accept the Iraqis, the news from London wouldn't help.

The river was my escape from the world. Once the trip was over, I would need to face the grimness of a world quite different from the one I'd left behind a day or so ago. But for a few hours, a couple of days, mine was the bliss of knowing nothing.

The canoe slid back into the river almost as if it, too, wanted to be away from the world; almost as if it had bonded with the river. The paddling seemed easier for some strange reason. Those thoughts were ridiculous, I told myself, don't be so stupid, inanimate objects are just that—inanimate. The river, however, was another thing. Like someone's house on the third or fourth visit, gradually it had become more comfortable for me and with me.

In the two days, 70 kilometres had gone by, and I felt good enough to try for a hundred before day's end. That would mean another four hours of easy paddling—easy being the operative word—which was not only my intention but all I could manage.

I passed more beaches, as well as other places, such as Bullanginya Lagoon and the Riversdale property, that had pumps, windmills, tanks, sheds for haystacks and machinery both old and new all visible from the water.

A couple of cabins appeared on the bank where a solitary fisherman sat under a bare willow tree and called out. Our conversation, about everything in general and nothing in particular, continued long after I had passed, our voices carrying through the emptiness.

The banks of the river were almost one continual beach approaching Tocumwal; Bourchier's, Boomagong, Moore's, White's, Clem's—there were as many beaches as there were bends. I knew that White's Beach was named after the family that farmed nearby, presumably so were the other beaches with Anglo-Saxon names.

The river bent one way and then the other, constantly. My backside was numb as the pillow was losing its effect, and my knees were desperately in need of some movement, so I stopped at the bank and headed off through the bush to stretch my legs.

A few minutes later I saw through the trees, backed up to a fence, a strange looking machine—a shiny amphibious vehicle with wheels up to my chest and a cover over two rows of seats for passenger protection. It would have looked like a prehistoric monster as it made its way through the forest and over the sandbars to slip into the water. Still, it looked like good fun, and if the river was good enough for houseboats and paddle-steamers, then what could be wrong?

A sign on the fence welcomed me to the Bushlands on the Murray Holiday Park, and Stuart Loe greeted me. If his black hair were any shorter he'd have been bald, while his piercing eyes and a torso that indicated hours spent in a gymnasium made him appear more menacing than he actually was. A builder by trade, he'd bought the bush block about fifteen years earlier after seeing it on a waterskiing trip. He and his wife had built the park bit by bit and hoped that soon he could give up building completely. We examined the chrome monster as he defended the use of speedboats on the river. He thought the erosion they caused was minimal. Stuart's theory was that when the river rose to a certain level it washed underneath the existing high watermark and cut away the soft sand from beneath the top of the bank, which was supported by tree roots and grasses and the like. He argued that this overhang eventually fell. Arguing was useless. Stuart did concede that the number of campers on the river didn't help much, that not all of them took away their rubbish, that they used the river for all manner of other reasons, and that many skiers didn't abide by the speed limits posted on trees along the banks.

After a bit more conversation I headed back through the bush to the canoe. With my body feeling much looser I resumed my journey with the intention of finding somewhere a little less commercial to camp. A couple of bends later I paddled under the Tocumwal Bridge.

Tocumwal had been part of the planned front-line defence of Australia during World War II. A theoretical line was drawn between Brisbane and Melbourne to mark the area that troops were confident could be defended against the Japanese forces. Called the Brisbane Line, there were a number of large airfields built along it, one of which was at Tocumwal. At the time, this was the largest airfield in the Southern Hemisphere and was set up for American heavy bombers to be used against the Japanese. Covering 25 square kilometres, the airfield was set up in four-teen days and had 100 kilometres of roads, four runways and a 200-bed hospital hidden in the forest. Over seven thousand American servicemen spent time there during the war. When the Japanese advance was halted the Americans moved north to Townsville. The aerodrome was eventually closed in 1960.

As inviting as the town looked, I decided to keep going. The earlier rejuvenation of my body had worn off, and my head was now throbbing. The novelty of paddling was wearing thin, and what I really needed was a quiet place to camp.

Rounding a bend, a figure in the distance at the far end of Forest Beach was swinging an axe. His arms crashed the blade downward and a second or so later the noise reverberated across the water. He stopped when I hauled the canoe as far up the bank as possible, then peered inquisitively at me before resum-ing his labour. It was still and quiet and the rain was about to fall. My bones were cold, my mind awash with weariness and his fire, although smoky, looked inviting. He might have seen my distress for he called out and walked over. 'Not much point havin' two fires,' he said. 'Throw yer swag in up here, it's a bit wet to frig around there.'

Pete, who didn't divulge his surname, was of a similar age to me, but was shorter, stouter and balder. He was right, it was a bit wet, or was going to be in the very near future. His caravan was like him—battered—but it did have an annexe, or at least the top half of an annexe.

We sat on camp chairs at the edge of the canvas annexe from which the rain fell in steady drips. Pete's hand disappeared into an old fridge laying on its side and emerged with a beer.

'Catch.' He threw it the metre or so between us.

Twisting the top off his own, he looked deep into the fire. 'Good to have someone to talk to.'

Although I was curious, something told me not to quiz Pete about his life, especially after I asked where he was from.

'Here and there,' he answered, not looking at me.

So instead we talked about football, cricket, and how the world would be better served by playing sport than by bombing itself into stupidity.

Eventually, Pete noticed my tiredness, and suggested we should have one last stubbie, after which he opened the door to the caravan, which swayed as he entered. I slid into my swag, alone with the patter of an occasional raindrop on the canvas, and wondered about the mysterious Pete.

Next morning Pete cooked breakfast while I sat nearby and moaned about being stiff and sore. When paddling everything was loose and working, but once I stopped it all seized up. Shoulders, arms, wrists, back—all were creaking. And, oh, those knees!

'What you need is a swim,' Pete informed me.

The water looked less than inviting and, although the morning had a certain warmth when standing in the sun, a swim was not high on my list of priorities. Instead I settled for a shower behind Pete's tarpaulin, where a tin with holes in the bottom swung from a tree. That was followed by a short stroll through the woodland to psyche myself up for the new day. An hour later I bid Pete farewell.

A low mist hung over the river, giving the trees and river an ethereal appearance. I would have appeared as a ghostly figure coming out of the gloom. Despite the outlook, the rhythm of the paddles and the soft plip as they entered the water returned like old friends. For a few seconds, thoughts of how easy it all was crossed my mind, thoughts which were banished almost instantly. I needed to keep myself in order and my mind concentrated. My pace was slowing but as long as my mind was willing, my body could afford to be a bit weak.

In some obscure way, I preferred the clouds. The river in winter appealed to some inner instinct. It was the attractiveness of the light, the way the overcast conditions brought out or emphasised certain colours, the creams and pinks of the bark, the greens and the browns, and, intermittently, the sound of the raindrops on the water and on my hat.

I had worked out a way to keep my legs from going numb and my back from seizing up completely. Stretching forward for a few strokes and then back, I created a callisthenic rhythm similar to my paddling stroke. It was difficult, but it eased the monotony and if I talked to the river and sang songs to myself the time passed. It reminded me of the part in *Waiting for Godot*, when one tramp says to the other, 'that passed the time'. To which the other replied that it would have passed anyway.

Meanwhile, the countryside was becoming more desolate and remote the further I travelled. There were still quite a number of beaches but fewer signs of population. After a couple of hours, Wide Beach and Doctor's Beach, Long Beach and Pump Beach had all disappeared behind me. At times the river and I were away from mankind even more than I imagined, some of the forests being inaccessible to anyone but those on foot.

At Ulupna Island in the Barmah State Park, dense red gum forests lined each bank and the Paddy Hennessey Cutting made me wonder about who Paddy was and why he had a cutting named after him. I was becoming a bit stir crazy by now, and to keep from losing my mind in the monotony of paddling, I made up stories about Paddy, fantasising that he was a bushranger who had been swallowed by a giant cod, and other such ludicrous things. Even though the river was in the best condition it could be for my trip, or at least at its most helpful, I hoped the end would come soon. My body implored me to stop, but I knew that if I did then tomorrow would be an even longer day. I plugged on as far as the Bunyip Hole on Snake Bend, where I decided that I'd done enough.

After dark I set off into the forest. It was wet underfoot and avoiding puddles required footwork sometimes more nimble than I could manage. Eyes shone back at me from the trees, staring into the light cast by my torch. A tawny frogmouth stared unblinking from a forked branch, convinced he was invisible. Kangaroos bounded in all directions, accompanied by the occasional screech of a bird and a swishing in the undergrowth as something ran from my approach. A cool wind wafted through the air.

When white men came to this country, Aborigines warned them about the bunyips who lived in waterholes and destroyed everyone who camped near them. Bunyips take many forms in the Dreamtime and in this thick, emotive silence, now broken only by the beating of my heart, I could sense one close at hand. Perhaps it was simply tiredness that made me emotional, but I was lonely that night, alone and lonely.

I was exhausted physically and felt the presence of the spirits. Perhaps those circumstances accentuate self-examination. I thought about my life. About where I was and where I was headed.

By morning most of the clouds had lifted. Those that hadn't were white and fluffy, not angry and black. With the expectation of finishing I felt much better, and as I pushed off, the current was swift and the paddling felt easier than it had been, helped along by a gentle breeze at my back. The river had lost its beaches and instead there were creeks heading off everywhere. House Creek, Gulf Creek, Pinchgut Creek.

I stopped at Sixty Mile Bend, which was just downstream from Bull Paddock. I didn't know where the bend was 60 miles from and working it out was too difficult so I simply sat on the bank, had a drink and prepared myself for the last 20-odd kilometres.

By the time the Edward River headed off to the right, Picnic Point was not far away.

Late winter

Picnic Point to Torrumbarry

The *Kingfisher* tourist boat, owned and operated by Benita Lamond, was a small, flat-bottomed craft that held about twenty people. Business was slower in winter, and on this trip there was only myself and a young couple.

After training as a park ranger Benita had begun driving the boat five years earlier and purchased the business when the opportunity arose. On a day when the only sounds, apart from us, came from nature, it was easy to see why. As soon as we pulled away from the bank, information from her special commentary was steadily forthcoming as we began our cruise through a unique part of the Murray River—the Narrows.

Twenty-five thousand years ago the Murray flowed north of its current path. The Goulburn River—which joins the Murray some 30 kilometres downstream from Picnic Point—flowed along the Murray's present course. A gigantic earth-quake caused what is known as the Cadell Tilt, damming the Murray and Goulburn and forming a large lake. Around eight thousand years later the Murray eventually broke through the lake. Its old course is now known as the Edward. The new section is the Barmah Choke, or the Narrows, much narrower than any other part of the river and named not only because of its restricted size but because of its limited capacity to carry water.

Because the Narrows is basically a new part of the river it doesn't have banks as such and during floods the water overflows into the Barmah Forest in Victoria and the Millewa Forest in New South Wales. These forests contain flora and fauna that would normally be found only in places with rainfall three times as great. Over thousands of years the water has helped create the largest stand of river red gums in the world. But the river doesn't flood much anymore.

Remains of trees sliced off just above the ground appeared at regular intervals, remnants of the days when paddle-steamers needed to load up if they were running low on fuel or when the loggers worked close to the water. Woodcutters used to cut lengths of red gum around a metre and a half in length and stack them every fifty or so kilometres beside the river for paddle-steamers to pick up. If the woodcutter was not around then steamers would give a blast from the whistle to indicate they would pay the next time through. (One woodsman became sick of his pile being stolen so he planted sticks of dynamite in the pile for when the culprit next came past. The resulting explosion soon fixed matters.)

The forest was the main source of wood for the Port of Echuca. Paddle-steamers from the river town towed huge out-riggers and barges upstream which, when loaded, were set adrift to float down with the current. A chain dragging behind kept them in midstream by digging into the sandy bottom on the bends and then straightening them out.

Paddle-steamers consumed close to a tonne of wood each hour of a 12-hour running day. About six tonnes were needed for a 16-kilometre trip. As well as that, the railways were expanding rapidly, requiring thousands upon thousands of sleepers. Then there was the tram system in Melbourne, which used blocks of red gum for the roadway. Ironically, by carting wood for the railways, which would be used for transportation, the paddle-steamers hastened their own demise.

At one time both the Barmah and Millewa forests were in danger of being completely demolished, but in 1909 the area on both sides of the river was declared a reserve. Of course, those regulations only worked to an extent; while Victoria bought back many logging licences years ago, on the New South Wales side of the river loggers can still basically do what they like.

One tree we passed had the fading figures '263' carved into its trunk. This was one of the rare old 'mileage trees', marked by the surveyor Pearce in his 1870 survey.

As the motor droned and the commentary came and went, I drifted off and watched the river life. A patch of giant rush, used by Aborigines for baskets and fish traps, grew near the bank where two pelicans watched imperiously as we chugged along. A darter was perched on a snag with wings outstretched. On rainy or overcast days darters spend most of their time drying their wings so they won't be too heavy to take off. A small kingfisher dipped and hid in the bare willows, the winter sun flashing off its blue back. A couple of wood ducks flapped madly as they left their hiding place and headed into the open. Up ahead, two cormorants played around our boat, flying and dipping into the water in front of us. High in a tree a mess of sticks clung desperately between the branches. Its owner, a white-bellied sea eagle, circled high above. These eagles, Benita explained, lived wherever there was a great supply of water and fish. The female will start a nest and continue to use it over a five-year period. This one watched us until it made sure we were leaving, then returned to its work. A water rat clambered along a snag in the middle of the river. He slipped into the water at one end, surfaced, looked around, then ducked under and returned near the snag. Then he did it again. It was a joyful day for water rats and humans alike.

There were other sights, though, not as endearing. At one point we passed a clump of arrowhead weed, one of the many curses now inflicted on the river. Arrowhead can't be dug out, nor can it be poisoned; nothing works, it just chokes up the waterway. Another was a patch of duckweed, which caused untold problems in waterways, although with work, according to Benita, that could be tamed.

The river widened again, and with Picnic Point just ahead, we turned. As we headed back, a little faster and a little quieter, Benita admitted to talking to the river and to her boat when they were alone. 'Amazing, isn't it?' she said. 'Having a conversation with a boat or a river.'

I smiled to myself and nodded.

The last part of the trip was completed in silence. As we pulled into the bank Benita pointed out 'Cobby's Tree'. More gnarled and wrinkled than any in the forest, it was named after a logger who once lived under it and loaded the steamers as they came down the river. He liked to drink methylated spirits and one night, after imbibing too much, spilled the bottle and stumbled into his campfire. They say some nights you can still hear the screams.

Benita docked the boat at her small mooring and, after everyone had gone, I stayed and watched the river for a while then walked along the bank and into the forest. In amongst the bark and sticks and weeds and native grasses were saplings ready to launch themselves upwards when the weather warmed up.

Sitting on a fallen trunk for a while, I took in the trees. Some, indeed many, were straight and tall and reached for the sky. A few were older, wiser trees with burls on their trunks and branches at ungainly angles, grown that way when there was more room. They reminded me of grandfathers with bunions who would sit quietly among the younger more vibrant of their offspring, not saying much, but taking it all in, hoping the younger ones would grow and learn and survive. But would these grow old and full of burls? In five hundred years' time would there be anyone to reflect on how it was before?

The moment was shattered by the arrival of a four-wheel drive with a boat on its roof secured by iridescent pink tie-downs. Thundering to a halt near the water, the door was pushed open and out of the cabin flew two small, yapping dogs that scurried around in circles alternately burrowing and jumping. The forest shook with rage; the silence embracing me crashed to the ground and splintered like a broken mirror.

Col Walker, a local Yorta Yorta tribal elder, had agreed to meet me in his office in Barmah near the edge of the forest. A man of seventy-one, Col's face was free of lines and wrinkles, his hair had only glimpses of grey and his grip was firm.

He showed me the pictures on his office wall. One was of a black cricketer, Sampson Barber, with a beard as bushy as W.G. Grace, (the English cricketer of the nineteenth century), a bat of the same vintage and pads that barely reached his knees. He wore a peaked cap, his shirt was done up to the neck and his trousers were pin-striped blue. Behind him were palm trees, put there to enhance the photo, but adding nothing to the cricketing scene. Sampson's eyes stared at me from the photograph, straight and proud. 'He was me Auntie Liz's uncle,' said Col.

Next to Sampson was William Cooper, a man who set up the Aboriginal Advancement League in Melbourne.

Col then pointed to a picture of a white man, his black wife, and their children. 'That's my great-grandmother and her husband,' said Col. 'Scotsman, I think.'

Col had been brought up by his grandmother after his mother died when he was seven. His grandmother was the first black woman to be a midwife in the area. 'She went up and down the river on the steam boats delivering babies, black and white, on stations, on the river, everywhere.' She also arranged with the riverboats to take people who had died back to their families.

Next along the wall was a photo of a football team taken not in the usual formal lines with arms folded, but with the players standing as though gathered and snapped in a hurry. 'That's the old Cumeragunja Mission team,' Col said, as proud as those in the photo appeared.

There were a number of Aboriginal missions built in the river area, one of the first being at Maloga in 1874, with another set up during the 1880s at Cumeragunja. Col had heard stories from before he was born about a man named Matthews, a Christian so-called Protector of Aborigines, collecting his family and many other Aborigines and taking them down to Maloga, later transferring them to Cumeragunja.

Life on the river was becoming crowded at the time, with white people encroaching on the traditional hunting grounds and making laws that told the Aborigines where they could and couldn't live, how and where they could hunt and fish.

'They just turned up, put up fences and signs saying "keep out, private property",' said Col, 'and they expected us to be happy with that.'

Col was born on the mission and lived there most of his life. He left school after third grade and worked with his father in the shearing sheds, then later on farms, never venturing far from home. He remembered the welfare people turning up at the mission to inspect living quarters, checking cupboards for food. Col laughed. 'We didn't need to have our cupboards full of food, we had a big supermarket out the front, fresh food every day.'

Col and some of the younger people still hunted, although they couldn't use traditional methods. He found it strange they were not allowed to use spears to catch kangaroos, nor were they permitted to build fish traps. Yet they could use guns to shoot and boats with coughing, spluttering motors to fish. And when they fished, he added, they didn't waste any. Not for them a boat full, they only took what they needed. It was the same with kangaroos and emus, just a couple at a time.

Col did not consider himself a radical, but he had a deep concern for his people and the way they had been treated. He rummaged through his files and showed me a photocopied piece of paper. It was from 1881, when his great-grandfather and forty-two others sent a petition to the government complaining that animals like cows and sheep were coming into their hunting grounds along the river and disturbing the forest. 'They never did anything about it. They did what they wanted to.'

For a few minutes Col's mind lingered in the past. He told me the river was their life, their blood, their water and food. 'It's a protector as well as our provider, old people would tell us to come home along the river, so the welfare couldn't get you; you could just swim across to the other side.'

The local Aborigines have many stories about the river and how it all began. The Yorta Yorta name for the river is Dhungalla. Col told me that during the creation period ancestral beings moved across the earth establishing the foundations of life. The most powerful of these was Biami.

Biami sent an old lubra down out of the high country with a yam stick to dig for food as she journeyed across the flat and waterless plain. He also sent his giant serpent to keep an eye on her. She walked for many weary miles drawing a line in the sand with her yam stick and behind her came the serpent, sliding in and out of the line and making curves of the river bed with his body.

Then Biami spoke in a voice of thunder, lightning flashed and rain fell, and the water came flowing down the track the old woman and the snake had made.

Col also spoke of the legend that described the river as a spine and the two nearby lakes as kidneys; out of those kidneys went the creeks and streams, veins giving life everywhere they went. He told me about their totem, the long-necked turtle. And how the wind and the call of a curlew at night meant bad news.

At the front of his offices we looked at a huge tree from which a canoe had been carved by Col's ancestors. The 'scar' tree had been shifted from the forest to keep it from danger. 'Beautiful, isn't it?' said Col, rubbing his hands gently over the ancient wood, the spirit of his ancestors alive in his eyes.

That night in the Barmah Forest, down near the water, I lay awake thinking about Col and his gentle philosophy. There was room for us all, he'd told me, we just need to be recognised and respected. I remembered his thoughts on racism; it was, he'd said, like electricity: you can't see it, but you know it when it hits you. I waited for the breeze to drop and hoped the curlews would be silent.

In Echuca the next morning, sitting amongst the paddle-steamers, I watched as lumps of red gum were piled onto a trolley for the PS *Canberra*. When the trolley was full the man dressed in old-fashioned overalls sent it, steadied by a length of rope, down the gangplank where his mate unloaded it.

Neil Hutchinson wore long sideburns and a moustache that curled at the ends in a matching pair of near-complete circles. He stood up and stretched as the trolley made its way towards the boat. 'Only twenty or thirty more loads to go,' he grinned.

His mate on board—the engineer Gary Aitken—was also hirsute, his black beard thick and wiry.

As they finished their work a few tourists turned up and I followed them down the gangway. Not long afterwards, a couple of steam whistle blasts were followed by the shudder of the decks as the idling engine kicked into gear, the huge paddle-wheels turned slowly on either side of the boat, and we eased away from the bank. Soon we steamed past the gigantic red gum wharf which was originally 330 metres long and built on three levels to accommodate the river's fluctuating height.

Moama, on the New South Wales side of the river opposite Echuca, was originally known as Maiden's Punt, after ex-convict James Maiden decided to take his stock and wool across the river there and send it to Melbourne, the closest big city. Later renamed Moama from the Aboriginal word for 'dead' because of the many graves in the area, it was established on its present site after the 1870 flood.

Soon afterwards Henry Hopwood, an ex-convict who had been transported to Australia at the same time as Maiden, set up across the river in Echuca. Hopwood was luckier than Maiden because, as this was where the Murray came closest to Melbourne, the railway arrived in 1864.

Echuca soon became the busiest port on the river where 'inside sailors'—as distinct from 'outside sailors', who were sea-going—came and went on hundreds of riverboats that brought goods from stations along the Murray and from other rivers such as the Darling and the Murrumbidgee. They brought with them wool, wheat and timber, and took back stores and machinery for the stations, together with shearers and others who needed transport. At one time there were 250 paddle-steamers and 700 barges working on the length of the river, most of which visited Echuca at some stage.

The town had its own breweries as well as about eighty pubs or wine bars. Impromptu horse races were held along streets where boutiques boasted the finest in women's fashion. Bare-knuckle fights took place on the riverbanks and legend has it that cod as big as a man were regularly caught.

Echuca is now home to the world's largest collection of paddle-steamers, one of which was the *Canberra*. Built in 1912, it had been refurbished only a few years before and had been at the forefront of the tourism boom related to the river and its boats. It wasn't the most beautiful of the steamers in Echuca, the *Emmylou* and the *Alexander Arbuthnot* arguably being more romantic due to their higher profile, but the *Canberra* was the only one that had worked on the river continuously since it had been built.

Neil swung the wheel around as we gave way to other craft, including the *Emmylou* on her way back to the wharf. A second-generation river man, Neil had done a few other things in his life here and there, but he knew he'd come back to the river. His father, the renowned river shipwright Kevin, had worked on many of Echuca's paddle-steamers. His latest project, the *Hero*, restored using old photographs as a guide, and old tools, was nearing completion. Kevin was even hand-forging the rivets that would hold the timber together. He'd been in love with the river and its boats for all of his sixty-four years and that passion had been passed on to Neil.

Leaving him to his navigation I climbed the ladder to the top deck where there was no one else, just the world and me. The steady slap of the paddles and the surge of the water from their sweeping circular motion were steady and reassuring. An hour or so later, after the tourists had disembarked, their photographs taken and their kids restrained once more, I joined the river brigade, taking the tinnie for a spin.

On my canoe trip there hadn't been much river traffic. Any boats that were around passed by during the day's break from paddling, or in the evening after I'd stopped. Here they were everywhere. Even though it was still late winter, the balmy weather lent itself to boating. In summer there would be many more, washing the water into the banks day after day.

Houseboats lined the banks. Some were homemade, some were replicas, others looked like they belonged in brochures about ocean-going yachts, only these didn't have the pointed prow or raised stern or large motors.

Lounging on the back of one were three young men, taking care not to tangle themselves in the many fishing lines hanging over the stern. More intent on drinking stubbies than fishing, they laughed hysterically at each other's jokes.

'They biting?' I called out.

'Wouldn't have a clue,' they yelled back and collapsed into more laughter.

I went downstream far enough to be alone and arrived at the Campaspe River junction. Walking along the banks, through the trees, watching the sheep in paddocks nearby, it appeared the river was happier. In Echuca it was almost resigned to its fate, but here it was free again.

It was late afternoon when I returned. The *Emmylou* was on its last trip for the day. The steam whistle sounded as it surged downstream, the passengers waving and smiling at me. I loaded the boat as the *Canberra* docked and wandered down the gangway. Their day's work completed, Neil, Gary and I sat on the stern. They laughed when I asked how special their life was.

'Special to everyone else, maybe,' said Neil, before correcting himself. 'It's good, really; I suppose you have to like it and be a bit eccentric to work with stuff nearly a hundred years old.'

The conversation turned to the river's health. Neil said that to him it wasn't that bad, that a lot of the noise about it was made by those with a political motive. 'If you want it to be buggered it can be,' he said. 'Sure there are things that have to be looked at, but most of those can be fixed by water and education—though we don't have a great deal of control over either of them.'

He also said that the problems at the bottom end of the river were unavoidable after it had drained about a seventh of the country. And much that was happening now had happened before. The mouth had been shut before. The river had stopped flowing before.

I changed the subject, keen to find out more about the *Canberra*. 'Any ghosts on the old girl?'

Neil and Greg were amused. 'Not that we know about, but it makes me laugh sometimes when I think about its history,' said Neil.

The man for whom the boat was built, David Connor of Boundary Bend, owned many boats on the river, some restored and still working. Connor was a temperate Salvation Army man, explained Neil, 'and now we have parties and blokes and women getting pissed and being sick—any ghost would not be impressed.'

The Connors would drive their Model T Ford onto the boat and go fishing. When the car was full with Murray cod, they'd drive it off and head to Swan Hill, where the fish were sold.

In later years, the Collins brothers from Mildura used the *Canberra* as a houseboat for a considerable time before it came to Echuca.

Neil dug out photographs from those times that showed gas lighting on the *Canberra*; the gas was produced from charcoal burned out of the forest's red gum. It all fitted beautifully. We cracked a can of beer and Neil said it was sad that there weren't many who really talked to the old blokes so a lot of the old river stories were lost. 'There's a fair bit of history been recorded but there's even more we don't know about.'

Inside, the engine hissed contentedly and Gary strolled over to check some gauges. The engine was built in 1923 and was once used to power a farm's water pump, then years later created steam for a drycleaner. It was still on huge steel wheels when they found it, but it was soon modified and slipped into the boat well.

'Engines like this are alive y'know,' said Gary as he wiped his oily rag across the brass.

He was right. There was a comforting, character-filled smell about the engine and the boiler. Oil and steam and grease have a way about them at the end of the working day. The pistons had stopped, the steam left the boiler with a sigh and the paddle-steamer had collapsed to the waterline. The pale sun had gone down behind the gum trees, which were silhouetted against the pink of the evening sky. The breeze dropped, the occasional bird screeched overhead, but apart from that the world was at peace.

I camped that night back at the Campaspe junction. It would have been good to stay in Echuca, but it was better to go, to be back out in the quiet, to hear the river again.

I was woken early the next morning by a combination of the dawn and the now familiar sound of birds. It was a much more pleasant way to start the day than trucks outside the windows and an alarm clock in my ear. Torrumbarry was only some 70 kilometres away according to my trusty *Murray River Charts* so it wasn't going to be a hard day. The boat was fuelled and the pillow on the seat had been replaced with one much more comfortable. I was now on the section that was the original Goulburn River. Neil had told me that the old river men called it the 'big Murray' when they reached this point again.

Along this part of the river, for every barren stretch of water there was an equal and opposite stretch that was full of houses. There was no one around anywhere except at the Deep Creek Marina where a couple of men were trying to start a motor. One would pull the starting rope furiously while the other one watched. When the first became frustrated the watcher tried his hand. Both had no luck apart from the odd quick roar that stopped almost immediately.

It was an uncomplicated trip, the easiest part so far, although the landscape was becoming flatter and less inviting. My book of charts told me this part of the river had many more interesting place names. First there was Dead Horse Point, then Sheepwash Lagoon, followed by the bends, Horseshoe and Turner, which came just before Dead Man's Hole. The last was Black Charlie Bend. I stayed there in honour of Col Walker— and Black Charlie, whoever he was.

Early spring

Torrumbarry to Swan Hill

When approval was given for its construction in 1919, the Torrumbarry Weir was to be the most upstream of twenty-six weirs and locks between the mouth of the Murray and the Port of Echuca that would enable navigation of the river under all conditions. When river trade diminished with the advent of railways, thirteen of the proposed weirs between Euston and Echuca were dropped from the plan. Now there are Locks 1 to 11 as well as Lock 15; Torrumbarry is Lock 26. It was never understood why the numbers didn't return to numerical order. Not that it mattered, but I wondered if anyone had ever got lost looking for Lock 20.

A twisting, narrow road lined by willow trees led from the highway to the weir, coming to an end near a caravan park in grounds as quiet and serene as you could wish for. Neat lawns and gardens under a canopy of trees surrounded the steel gates attached to brick pillars. A short walk through the gates and I was standing at the weir.

Initially, the weir consisted of a series of steel trestles along a concrete base that were hauled in and out of the river by a steam-driven winch. During spring a team of six men would take five days to put the fourteen trestles in the water for the summer's irrigation, with huge timber bars dropped into place to hold the water back so it could be fed out through the channel system. After nine months it would be winched out again for maintenance. The weir keeper lived close by, letting boats through the lock, keeping the upstream level constant, and removing snags that floated downstream.

Passing coach trade triggered the town's growth in the early 1900s and at one stage there were eight schools and several hotels. Bush nurses were the only health service and travelled on horseback to isolated areas. Most only stayed in the district a few years. All that's left of the once thriving town is the Torrumbarry Hotel on the highway with a petrol station nearby.

The weir took several years to complete and many complications arose during its construction, not the least of which were problems with the workers. Strikes over wages were commonplace, with one lasting twelve months. Another erupted over a food fight. Two waiters were flinging tomatoes at each other when a stray red missile hit the cook, an act that resulted in one of the waiters being sacked. The union was called in and tension increased until the police restored order.

This was not the last of the weir's troubles. In 1992 the weir was found to be severely damaged and leaking considerably. Repairs were carried out but they only delayed the inevitable. Construction on the new weir began in 1993 and it was opened four years later.

Torrumbarry was the last weir on the river for over 500 kilometres. From about 10 kilometres downstream to around the Murrumbidgee junction was where the river was closer to its natural state in terms of its flow: high flows in winter due to rains and low in the dry summer. Now, in summer the river is usually high with irrigation water when it should be quite low, while in winter, when flows would normally be higher, most water is captured by the dams and stored for the following summer. Of course, some water is let through in winter, not only to maintain a constant flow but because there would be floods if the water banked up behind the weirs.

Before returning to the river I had devised a plan to drive from the Torrumbarry Weir through the Gunbower State Forest to Koondrook–Barham, twin border towns downstream.

The forest was part of Gunbower Island, the largest inland island in Australia, bordered on one side by the Murray and on the other by the Gunbower Creek, which left the river just below Torumbarry and joined it again at Koondrook. The creek was another consequence of the Cadell Tilt.

My map of the forest showed a mass of lines—broken and unbroken—which looked like a large dish of spaghetti. The map's legend indicated that one of the lines was a forest track while another which looked extremely similar, was a *major* forest track. The difference escaped me, but I decided to take the designated tourist drive.

As it turned out, the tracks were surprisingly good, enabling me to zip along when the river wasn't in sight and slow down when it was. Away from the river the ground was dry grey dirt, mudflat country. Box trees grow well in that sort of soil whereas red gums like more water. Further along the trees became thicker and the tracks more difficult to follow. At every corner there seemed to be a small wooden post that named a track. Unfortunately, the posts didn't have any arrows pointing the way and I'm an arrow kind of bloke. But a few missed turns and a misreading of the map were just glitches in an otherwise perfect day. Spring in this part of the country was sublime. On the back of my map—which actually had the drive marked in bold lines so it was easier to follow—was information about the fauna and flora in the forest—one hundred and seventy species of birds, twenty-four reptile species, and around two hundred different sorts of plants.

Late in the afternoon I set up camp at Cemetery Bend. Close to the river were the graves of the two Mathers children, daughters of the people who, in the 1880s, managed the 100 Mile timber mills, so named as it was 100 miles from Echuca. The children were believed to have drowned in the river. A white picket fence around the graves was achingly visible through the trees and that night I hoped the Mathers children had, like me, watched the stars sparkle across the water.

In the morning I walked beside the river for a while. During holiday times there would be scores of people and camps all along the river and through the forest. Now there was only me. Many years before, much like the holiday times, the population was considerably greater.

The Barababaraba tribe were the first inhabitants of the area. They called the place Kanbowro, which meant 'twisted and tortuous', like the necks of the black swans that once glided on the river, the creeks and lagoons.

By chance, I came across a scar tree and a midden and wondered whether it was fate or whether the river had directed me to this place. It was as though I'd found a footprint frozen in time, left by someone who trod here thousands of years before.

The forest was the second biggest stand of red gums in the world, after Barmah–Millewa. The trees along the river were all reasonably young, having replaced those cut down because it was easier to haul them from here straight to the steamers and barges. The older trees were much safer, further into the forest.

In the early days a couple of sawmills worked in the forest. At one stage there was even a school that catered for the children of the mill workers. Robson's Mill, started in 1875, once stood a short distance from my camp and was a big producer of sleepers for the railway system that would eventually kill off the steamers. As well as the local men others worked in the forest—the swagmen of the river, the Murray Whalers.

During the Great Depression scores of these men had left the cities looking for work. Many had been reasonably successful in their chosen careers but with hard times, and many other swaggies on the road, they had taken to the rivers, eking out whatever sort of existence they could. They each had a wooden rowing boat in which was usually found a dog, a tent, kerosene lamps and the like. It was easier to stash that amount of stuff in a boat than to carry it around on your back. Their road was the river and their verge the riverbanks. They survived on fish, rabbits, foxes, galahs, even the occasional plunder of a sheep. They travelled most of the Murray's length and worked for anyone who would help them.

An idyllic life, perhaps, but one in which the romance would soon wear thin. Some of them worked in the sawmills when they could, either cutting timber with an axe or as sniggers, the men who brought the fallen trees to the mill. Not many went back to their old lives when the hard times finished. Perhaps they were content with the river and the space and the freedom.

At the end of my forest drive was the only timber mill left in the forest, Arbuthnot's in Koondrook, started in the 1870s by Alexander Arbuthnot. (I had seen the paddle-steamer named after him in Echuca.) Called Sandy as both his father and son were also Alexander, he was committed to his work, so much so that he married on Christmas Day because that was the only day he would take off.

At its peak the enterprise employed some two hundred men—fellers, sniggers, mill workers, haulers, ship builders and those on steamers specially built to transport the timber. Arbuthnot's owned the *Koondrook*, the largest barge ever on the river, which was capable of carrying 200 tonnes.

The sawmill still operated from the place where it was founded. Timber now came and went on huge semitrailers that pulled in close to the river a short distance from where the wharf once stood. The sawmill sheds hadn't changed much over the years but the huge logs are no longer loaded by men with pulleys but by a forklift with wheels taller than a man. A truck was waiting to be relieved of its load, and the driver—who had a build similar to one of the logs he was carting—was also the driver of the forklift which had just lifted a log with a girth wider than I was tall off the truck.

'Gotta do everybloodything!' he yelled over the noise. The driver reckoned everyone he knew was a conservationist. 'Not bloody stupid like some of 'em but we know what we're doing.' For fear of being critical, I didn't quiz him about what he meant.

He was behind schedule so I left, walking back out of the gates past a life-size red gum statue of Sandy, carved with a chainsaw.

Even with my studying of the river I needed clarification on a few points, so home in Swan Hill I visited a mate who I knew would have answers to my questions. Peter Koetsveld worked on the water authority that had control of the river between Torrumbarry and the Nyah Forest, some 300 kilometres downstream. I'd known Peter for many years and knew that he enjoyed a special relationship with the river. Helping me to understand how they regulated water in the river, he explained how the weirs created a series of steps up from the mouth to the Hume Dam, then showed me large maps with more coloured lines than in a kindergarten painting class. The Murray was, he said, a huge artery running across the country with capillaries and veins leading from it, delivering water to a thirsty land. Much more than just a water carrier, it was an incredibly powerful living thing, giving life to a large proportion of the continent.

All along the river I'd come across different views on how good or bad the river was depending on what happened in the area I was visiting. Upstream they had said they didn't have much to worry about, but here in the middle reaches there were real problems.

Peter, a small man with bad taste in both politics and football teams, gave me his views on the river's health. He'd been brought up on an anabranch of the river—the Marraboor, as the Aborigines knew it, or Little Murray to the white man. In those days, he said, the river was clear and when fishing you could see the redfin chasing spinners as you reeled them in. Now, he said, you're lucky if you can see anything. We laughed about the childhood game of standing in the weeds and letting leeches attach themselves to our legs, then getting out and picking them off. On really hot days you could turn them inside out on a piece of wire and fry them on the bitumen. No more. Even the leeches have left.

Apart from lack of water due to ongoing droughts, one of the problems facing the river, according to Peter, was the drainage it collects. 'It comes from everywhere and the further downstream the more it gets.' Imagine, he said, all the farms and towns and creeks and small places that drain into the Murrumbidgee and the Darling. 'All their detergents, poisons, fertilisers, chemicals, and such like end up in the river. There's run-off from bad farming practices like excess tillage. Not to mention salt that rises through the earth when farming land is cleared of trees.' Then there was overgrazing by stock and pest animals which meant important plants such as river red gums weren't reproduced. Clearing land for grazing also destroyed plant life causing more run-off that, together with animal wastes, ensures more nutrients drain into the river.

Peter said that in his experience most farmers are aware of the problems and have changed their attitude to a large degree, although there was still much to do. As Neil Hutchinson in Echuca said, drain a seventh of the country and what do you expect.

One school of thought was that the river had never been better, mainly because salinity was dropping, but Peter said that salinity levels always varied when water came from the alpine catchments. 'Then, if we get flows from the more saline country, it goes up.' According to Peter, there was still a big problem with salt. Among other drains in this part of the country, he singled out Barr Creek, which drained all the saline land around the district back into the Murray. Nearly 150 000 tonnes of salt goes into the river each year.

Most of the problems could be fixed with more water, which could be used to flush the river—but, as Peter asked rhetorically, 'Where do we get the water from?' Part of the answer as he saw it was controlling the amount of water farmers could use. 'In bad years they are not allowed to use all their water allocation,' he said. 'It can get down as low as 50 per cent and, if there were years of continuing bad droughts, theoretically they may not be allowed any. Then we'd all be in big trouble.'

The Swan Hill section of the river—around 100 kilometres upstream and downstream of Swan Hill—is the only place where the Murray River is still in its natural state. Or at least as close as is possible. There are not as many houseboats, paddle-steamers or, indeed, people here as there are in places with levels regulated by weirs, but the area has its own unique qualities. Beyond the influence of the Torrumbarry Weir and the next weir downstream at Euston, the Murray in this vicinity rises and falls regularly in the way it once did.

Ted Ward owned a paddleboat in Swan Hill. The *Iron Dry* was not a houseboat, nor was it a steamer, just a small, diesel-powered replica riverboat with paddlewheels on each side and a sparse but comfortable interior. Despite not being soaked in the watered history of the river, and even though it was only built a few years previously, it had character, nevertheless. Her sixty-year-old engine had once powered a double-decker London bus, which lent her a certain degree of nobility.

For many months Ted and I had planned a trip up the river, discussing when to go, working out how many bottles of whisky we'd need and whether we'd actually come back. Eventually we settled on a date and, late one afternoon, we chugged out of the small marina that was home to about five other, more elegant, houseboats. With Ted setting the engine at a steady six knots we headed, slowly but comfortably, upstream.

With the river level higher than normal we could see across the plains and through the paddocks. Ted's opinion was that at the other, more regulated parts, the river was like a duck pond, the same height all the time. Here, though, levels changed regularly, dramatically at times, and the current could be very slow or very quick depending on the amount of water coming down. Around here, he said, you can see the river's true character. When the river is low there are always big problems but when it is like this, said Ted, there is nothing better anywhere. Another plus, we agreed, was that there were no speedboats on this stretch of the river, no one whizzing past on jet skis, only the occasional tinnie, and very little noise.

As the paddle-steamers did, we tied up in the twilight. Unless there was a full moon, or on odd occasions when their searchlights were used because they needed to work, it was always dangerous for them to travel at night. I secured the boat with ropes around a big gum tree a little way downstream from a sharp bend.

As evening closed in and the sun dropped from the sky, the kookaburras began their evening calls. The river gushed swiftly around the bend and over the logs that lay in large numbers along the banks. Ducks quacked their way home and the light breeze eventually tired.

On the stern we threw out a couple of lines in the forlorn hope of luring a fishy meal and watched the last vestiges of light as they played their daily game with nature. The willows' new green tinge shone and the red gums, tall and strong, became contorted and black against the blue left after the sun had vanished. The sky was a kaleidoscope of blues, whites and pinks, the swirls of the clouds reflecting those of the river. Early stars hung as though pinned to a ceiling. Silhouettes abounded, from the fishing rods poked out through the guardrail to the lone bird floating across the sky, from the intricate patterns of leaves against the light to the dead twisted fingers of the branches on the snags. The trunks of the trees that lined the banks bent in almost irregular patterns that had nothing, yet everything, in common. A swallow's chirp, the squawk of three ducks that flew in formation, and the sound of cicadas filled the night air.

Ted was bony, his wrinkled face inscribed by his years as a mallee farmer. A smoke was never far from his smiling mouth. By his own admission a somewhat eccentric soul, Ted had lived near the river for all his sixty-three years. In 1893 his grandfather selected land at Woorinen, about five miles inland from Swan Hill and six miles in a direct line to the Murray. Ted remembered his grandfather's stories about the droughts in the early 1900s, when many Mallee farmers would take horse and drays on a day-long trip to the river for water. Tanks would leak on the way home and, by the time the horses had drunk their fill, it was almost time to return for more. Ted's farming interest now was vineyards, which continued his family's reliance on the river—although these days, he told me with a grin, it was a bit easier.

Even though it was something of an extravagance, the *Iron Dry* had given Ted and his family—not to mention friends—many days of pleasure.

'There's no question about being on the river doing something for you,' he said. 'You can be anywhere with any problems but when you are on the river it has a charm, a seduction almost.' Ted reckoned the river was the best psychiatrist in the world and much cheaper than those more qualified. 'It's great therapy, no doubt; and there's no hurry.'

Which was just as well, as six knots doesn't get you very far. But then we had no real plan for the trip, nor any real destination. Just a few days on the river, travelling slowly, enjoying whatever there was to offer.

Ted lit the barbecue and I opened the whisky. We had been away for four or five hours and we had not seen anyone or anything. We were probably only 10 kilometres from home but we were a million miles from society.

In the morning mist hung over the water like a shroud. The river had risen even more overnight, the result of rain upstream flowing into the river and from an overflow out of Torrumbarry. That, combined with melting snow in the highlands, meant the river was at its finest.

After breakfast Ted set our course and we trundled along, methodically, reassuringly, steadily. We soon came upon a house close to the water's edge and a couple of blasts on the whistle brought children rushing down to the bank just as children did when real steamers plied the river. My imagination ran wild. I could see figures in the dew-covered native grasses that spread away towards the paddocks, and sensed old riverboat captains around me. I stared at the trees on the bank and wondered how some of them could possibly stay upright. The roots of one appeared like a spider on tiptoes, while others less fortunate had succumbed to the erosion and dropped into the water, lying prostrate like so many Goliaths.

On the bank below some willow trees, a rusty hulk was tied to a temporary mooring. Under the layers of different coloured metal was a paddleboat, although not quite what would normally be construed as a paddleboat. The owner had laid out the hull, driven an old tractor on board, removed the machine's back wheels and attached extensions onto which paddles were fixed. A few sheets of iron were welded over the top and there it was— a brown, green, grey and silver pleasure contraption.

Half an hour later we came upon a sign. Unlike most others on the river, which politely advised people to 'Keep Out—Private Property', this one simply stated, in huge red lettering, 'Piss Off!' Not wanting to tempt fate by stopping, we chugged on.

There was very little of the river that was straight. The curves and turns were almost continuous. Around one of them we pulled into a camp set up by a few Swan Hill men. Camps like this were reasonably prevalent along the river. An escape from the everyday life, it had a couple of old caravans, some almost wrecked chairs, electricity hooked up to a generator, an old refrigerator on its side and logs dragged over to the fire to serve as seats and firewood.

We enjoyed a drink or two that soon led to three or four, and more. We listened to stories that would not be repeated in good company—or any company for that matter, other than that we were in.

The revelry and competitive drinking soon became decidedly dangerous for our health so we untied and the engine quickly resumed its methodical throb. I gave up my position behind the wheel to Ted and sat on the stern. This was the way to travel, I decided, as my hand trailed over the side, fingers sliding through the water. The day was alive; the sun was on my face and dancing on the water. It was a *Wind in the Willows* kind of day. Ah, Toad, Ratty, you had it right, didn't you? There's nothing quite like messing about in boats.

We didn't see many people; even those in the houses we came across were mostly unseen. We had two lots of visitors who pulled up for a chat when they saw us and wanted to know what we were doing. Each night we talked a lot of rubbish, and drank and ate too much.

After a few languid days we reached Pental Island, another of the many places where the river split and flowed in two sections. This was where Peter Koetsveld had lived, the Marraboor—or Little Murray—River that left the big Murray here and returned at Swan Hill. The Marraboor, in turn, was joined by the Loddon, which brought water to the Murray from the centre of the state. For many years there was a dispute as to whether Pental Island was part of New South Wales or Victoria, but early last century Victorians proved to the Privy Council there was more water flowing on the south side than the north and were awarded the land.

Just upstream of Pental Island we turned back. The return journey was more hazardous, with both of us losing control when rounding bends such as the aptly named Funnell Bend, which almost funnelled us to disaster. The current was strong and if you didn't head into it correctly, the boat would be swept across the river and close to the bank. The old captains had these problems too, although with their skill they could always get out of them. Ted and I got through with luck more than anything else.

One house built on a bend had majestic views both upstream and downstream. I wondered aloud what it would be like to own something like that, with its waterfront mooring, its grass verge to the river's edge.

You never own land, Ted responded, 'you only pay for the privilege of looking after it'. And sometimes, he said, smiling as he looked out the front of his boat, you have the privilege of being on it and looking after it and it doesn't cost a cent.

Mid-spring

Swan Hill to Mildura

Dad found a new job and moved the family to Swan Hill in 1960, which is when the Murray became a huge part of our lives. The river was different then; everything was different. Sometimes after school, if there was no sport to be played, I would go fishing. Holding my fishing rod precariously on the handlebars I would ride my bike down to the river and try, with the aid of a worm or a shrimp, to entice a fish onto my hook. More often than not it was unsuccessful. If nothing was happening with the fish then I'd climb trees to look in birds' nests, catch lizards or skim stones, or swim from the sandbars. Later, when I was on leave from the navy, Dad and I would spend a day or two by ourselves fishing on the river—not that we ever caught much. It didn't matter, though. We were happy just to sit under the trees, listening to the rush of the wind through the eucalyptus canopy and talking about cricket and football, about life and death, about the taste of oranges warmed in the sun and the poetry of Siegfried Sassoon.

Major Mitchell named Swan Hill on 20 June 1836, during his trip along the Murray. Camped near the river, the sound from black swans on the slight western rise kept him awake. Close to the spot Mitchell camped are now two bollards, carved from red gum, depicting the riverboat captains who took up the South Australian government's offer to explore the river. In 1851, Governor Henry Fox Young offered £2000 each to the first two boat owners to successfully navigate the Murray from its mouth to the Darling River junction to open the rivers for trading possibilities. There were stipulations however. The boats had to be not less than 40 horsepower and their depth in water no more than 60 centimetres when fully laden.

Francis Cadell, an ex-Royal Navy man, had studied river navigation in America and was keen to try his luck. To find out more about the river he trekked to Swan Hill with a tent and a packhorse. He made his way via the Bendigo goldfields, where he hired three luckless miners who were about to return to Adelaide. In Swan Hill, Cadell and his men constructed a boat that looked like a large canoe from mallee timber. Called the *Forerunner* it was almost seven metres long, a metre wide and had a draft of half a metre. The timber frame was covered with canvas waterproofed with mutton fat. When he and the miners were about to leave, Cadell laid a pistol beside him in the boat—a none-too-subtle hint that he was the boss. A month later, with the assistance of sails at times but mainly rowing, he arrived home. After finding out what he wanted to know about the Murray, Cadell had his vessel built in Sydney and sailed the *Lady Augusta* round to Encounter Bay at the river's mouth.

William Randell, by contrast, was a young grazier who had never seen a steam boat before he built his own. He and his brothers had decided to take flour from their mill upstream to sell to the settlers along the river. Randell cut the timbers from his father's farm 50 kilometres away in the Mount Lofty ranges and took them to Noa No station near Mannum by bullock team. There he built and named the *Mary Ann*, the first paddle-steamer on the river. One of the more notable features of the *Mary Ann* was that she had an oblong-shaped boiler that swelled dangerously when fired. More rivets were added, and a large bullock chain was wrapped around it and lashed to the stern. The boat also had two masts and in some parts of the river sails were hoisted to assist their passage.

Randell set off up the Murray first but was soon overtaken by Cadell. At times the two captains raced each other before deciding this was a fruitless task; after that, each went about their voyage in their own way. Cadell arrived in Swan Hill on 17 September 1853, twenty-three days after leaving the starting point at Goolwa. Randell arrived some four hours later. The population of Swan Hill at that time was twenty-seven—twelve white people and fifteen Aborigines.

As they had not carried out exactly the required tasks set down by Governor Fox, neither man qualified for the government's grant, but they were rewarded nonetheless. Cadell received 900 guineas, Randell £300 and a purse of sovereigns. Both men then set up riverboat operations.

Later, in 1860, Swan Hill was one of the last staging points for the ill-fated Burke and Wills when they embarked on their epic journey to the Gulf of Carpentaria. They took with them Charlie Gray, an ostler from the local hotel, the Lower Murray Inn. Some historians have said that if it wasn't for Gray, Burke and Wills might have survived. Gray became ill on the return journey and they stopped to bury him. If they had not, then they might have reached Coopers Creek before the support party left. Gray was buried, with his hat still on, in a metre-deep grave.

Swan Hill became the first place in the country to recognise the importance of the early settlers with the establishment of the Swan Hill Folk Museum in 1963. Australia's first living, working outdoor museum, later renamed the Pioneer Settlement, it had a huge collection of items relating to the region's rural life spanning the years from 1830 to 1930, many of national and international significance. The Pioneer Settlement is still one of the largest outdoor museums in Australia. The centrepiece of the Settlement is the PS *Gem*, the largest paddle-steamer ever to ply the river. A passenger vessel, it operated all along the river, as far down as Goolwa and as far upstream as Echuca. When it was purchased by the museum, the *Gem* was in Mildura without a boiler and an engine, so it had to be towed to Swan Hill by a much smaller steamer, the *Oscar W*. The man charged with the trip was Paddy Hogg, owner of the *Oscar W* and the last of the true riverboat captains.

Paddy was christened Hilary Harding but those names didn't stick. An orphan, he was taken in by the Andersons, a riverboat family in Echuca. Charlie 'Swan' Anderson had earned his nickname because of his affection for a swan with a broken leg he had nursed back to health and which followed him around everywhere he went, on water or on land.

They made sure Paddy knew everything they could teach him about the Murray and soon he was known up and down the river. The Andersons, Paddy and all the other captains or riverboat men were 'Top Enders', the name given to those who plied the Murray upstream from Wentworth as well as those who journeyed up the Murrumbidgee and the Darling. 'Bottom Enders' were South Australians.

Paddy owned or captained many of the well-known riverboats during his life and was one of those river men who had a story for every part of the river, most of them true. Like many on the river he was jealously disliked by some but admired by all.

Paddy's son Bill, the third generation to have plied the rivers, now runs the *Kookaburra*, a tourist boat at Swan Hill named after one of the last commercial steamers his father owned. Bill, now sixty-five, had just turned twenty when he and his father took the original *Kookaburra* on what was believed to be the last commercial cargo run up the Murray, ferrying a load of stone from Waikerie to Mildura.

A few years later, Paddy sold the steamer to Lyle Bennett, who wanted to use it as a cabaret cruiser. Paddy delivered the boat to Bennett in Nyah with his then wife, Pearl Wallace, the first female riverboat captain.

Pearl was a legendary figure herself, being the inspiration behind Nancy Cato's book *All the Rivers Run*, later turned into the famous television series. Pearl's father and brothers were all riverboat captains and she had her first taste of the riverboat life when just three weeks old. When Pearl was granted her captain's licence the examiners told her she was as good as any man they had seen and better than some. She retired at sixty-six years of age.

On delivering the *Kookaburra*, Paddy and Pearl advised Bennett to look at the hull as it needed prompt attention. After a few weeks the river level at Nyah dropped and it became clear why the advice was given to Bennett. The snag on which the boat had apparently been resting went right through the wood. The *Kookaburra* lay in the river for years and many of her fittings, including the boiler and engine, were stolen. The new, steel-hulled *Kookaburra* would never have that problem.

Bill Hogg had spent his life on the river and, sitting on the deck of the *Kookaburra* tied up to his private wharf, remembered the early days with affection. After World War II, Paddy, his first wife, Bill and four daughters lived in a ramshackle hessian-walled place on the riverbank near Echuca at a place called Jeffrey's Swamp. When Bill's mum left, the girls went to other homes and Paddy and Bill moved to Morgan in South Australia.

Bill was eleven when Paddy decided it was time to teach him more about the river. They owned a flat-bottomed wooden boat that Paddy loaded with 'a camp oven, a fishing line, two rabbit traps, half a pound of tea, a pound of flour, and a bit of salt.' The idea was for Bill to row from Mildura to Renmark, a distance of around 200 river miles, which, Paddy estimated, would take a bit over two weeks. Facing downstream as did all men who rowed the river, and pushing, rather than pulling the oars, young Bill set off, the river, and all it held, in front of him.

'Took me ten days,' said Bill. 'I rang Dad from Renmark and told him where I was. He wouldn't believe me.'

In his laconic way, Bill said it was an idyllic time. Just a boy and his river, taking in the world around him. He fished at times; he camped at night in his homemade swag made of hessian and lined with sheepskin. He made friends with the birds and animals. There was no danger, no strangers—and even if there had been, they would have been like him, travellers on the river.

His lone rowboat journey taught Bill a great deal about river life, and on each trip with his father and the men on the steamers he learnt some more. Bill worked on the riverboats scrubbing decks and peeling potatoes among other tasks. He had little schooling. Every time his father tried to enrol him in some formal education Bill would run away and be found along the river somewhere, waiting for his father's steamer. 'He'd pick me up and give me a rollicking,' laughed Bill, 'and then try again a bit later.'

The *Kookaburra* was due to head off on its daily cruise and, as always, Bill was looking forward to the wonders of being on the river. 'This is my life, I can't get it out of me,' he said as we watched a couple of large sticks float by. 'It has its own special magic, it's alive.' Bill reckoned that most times he goes out he'd come across a tree or something else that reminded him of Paddy, whether it was one of his father's stories, or one from the other old blokes. One of his most treasured possessions, apart from the stories and the memories, was a river chart from 1865, created using calico and ink. Charts such as these were made by riverboat captains on one long scroll about 30 centimetres wide. Stored in the wheelhouse, the captains would wind them across as they steamed along the river. The charts were handed down and information exchanged. Every rocky bank, every woodpile, every sandbar and mileage tree on the river was marked carefully so others would be able to travel safely.

Bill looked wistfully at the river. 'He's always out there, the old man, perhaps it's a snag or a swirl or a corner where something happened. I'm the luckiest bloke in the world to know all that.'

Two days after bombs had shattered Bali for the second time, I spent a couple of days meandering along the river around Swan Hill in the tinnie. Although it was a relaxing, safe place to be I wasn't sure of my feelings. Apart from the papers and television, in this part of the country we were isolated from the war in Iraq, the bombings and other terrorist activities, which made it difficult to feel too bad. You tend to forget about things if they're not close at hand and if you have other distractions. Feeling a little guilty, I sat in the boat at peace with everything around me, immune to feelings of outrage, and guessed how many others would like to be with me.

I set off upstream under the Swan Hill bridge then, at the junction, turned along the Marraboor River towards my mother's house. Years before, when my father died, we had scattered some of his ashes in the river there. We hoped they might float down to Berri so he could retrace his steps, and so that a part of him could be at rest in the place he had brought us to. Despite never having been on the Marraboor in the boat I had watched it at times, hoping for inspiration and for a message of sorts. To indulge myself in some memories and to let Dad know that things were okay.

Heading back downstream, the river was familiar to me but this time I tried to look more closely, to see what hadn't been apparent before.

In the early days, Aborigines in the area had called this place 'martyrocquert', which means 'platypus'. Bill Hogg recalled two pairs on the river as recently as ten years ago. He said that one pair had simply disappeared. He didn't know what happened, although he was fearful for them, especially after the other pair were caught in a drum net and drowned. Bill laughed when I said that no one would ever have expected to see platypus around here. 'That's just another of the river's secrets not everyone knows.'

The rivers around Swan Hill had plenty of fish, though, including a 'Big Cod' near the railway station. Unlike the purpose-built 'big' things scattered all over the country to attract tourists, this was a leftover prop from a long-forgotten movie made about country life by people who had no idea what country life was actually like. The movie flopped but the Big Cod made countless tourists happy as they had their photographs taken while sitting in its mouth.

Fishing in the area was the best it had been for a long while. Cod were now in greater numbers than for many years, and fisher persons of all persuasions flocked to the area in the hope of catching a big one, which many did.

Murray cod are an ancient fish, indeed some skeletal remains have been found dating back twenty-six million years. Stories about them are unlimited, with fish sizes matched only by the size of the tales. Some say they have caught cod that were so strong they pulled the fisherman into the river. Another tells of a farmer who kept losing tackle to a monster cod and came back with bigger and bigger tackle until finally he used a kangaroo on a meat hook which was attached to his tractor by a steel cable. The cod won the battle and the wrecked tractor sits dejected under a red gum near the spot. Stories like these have kept people like me ever positive that one day it would happen; one day a cod would find its way onto the line. One day.

Up until 1917 there were very few trees along the banks around Swan Hill, due to the river's constant flooding. Now, with greater control of the river, some red gums have grown there. Most of them are, by red gum standards, quite young, many well under a hundred years old. However, further inland they are dying through the usual problems—salt, poisons and, most of all, no precious water flowing into the floodplains—and without those flood-plains, there is very little chance of the Murray ever being anywhere near the river it was once. Floodplains right along the river have been developed for agricultural and recreational purposes, dividing them from the river system. If they are lucky, those left are now covered with water every ten years or so, whereas for millennia they were flooded almost every second year.

Below the bridge the river was now wider, shallower and slower than upstream of Swan Hill. Indeed in the early 1900s the river had stopped flowing altogether. Before regulation the river was usually navigable for about eight months a year, although in the 1914–15 drought it was reduced to a series of ponds and it was two years before steamers could get up the river.

The region was known as the Swan Hill Plains. Fierce winds surging in from across the plains forced the steamers to tie up at night for fear of being blown off course. They could also get lost—on a high river in the days before levee banks, water would spread out across the plains and the main channel of the river would become impossible to see.

Alec Morrison was a boat captain who once had problems during a flood near Renmark. He had a particular taste for brandy and had been enjoying a drink with Paddy Hogg one night on the PS *Marion*.

Late in the evening Alec came upon Pollard's Cutting, a long sweeping bend, and made for a gap in the gum trees that he thought was the main channel. It wasn't and he became stuck. It took a couple of other boats to tow him off.

Alec was summoned to Melbourne to appear before the Water Authority Board who asked if he had been drinking. Alec denied the charge and said the moon was so full and so beautiful that he became mesmerised and the next thing he knew he was stuck out on the flats.

The investigating committee was suitably impressed by the story and Alec retained his licence.

The Murray is called the 'Slow River' for good reason. The slowest river in the world, it falls the least in altitude between mountains and sea and is the most winding. The fall of the river at Albury is around 14 centimetres per kilometre while during the last 160 kilometres of its journey the fall is only 2.5 centimetres. It flows slowly because of the gradient and because the evaporation rate in some places is higher than rainfall. Also, it flows through desert country that contributes very little water and, because it starts at such a low altitude compared with other rivers, the flow rate doesn't rise quickly. As it meanders it erodes one side of the river bank and deposits silt on the other, which slows it even more.

Around Swan Hill the land is at its flattest and over the years of turning and twisting to find a path the river has created numerous islands; Beveridge Island, for instance. Named after early settlers in the district, it was bounded by the Murray on both sides. The second of the streams was another to be called 'Little Murray', just one more of the river's countless anabranches.

When they settled the land in 1846, the Beveridge family had a reasonable relationship with the Aborigines of the area, but that soured when the black people killed sheep for their own use. Andrew Beveridge sent a black emissary with a message to the tribe that he would kill the next sheep thief. The tribe's response was to spear Beveridge to death. The government then sent three undercover police to take the killers into custody. After a short battle in which some tribesmen were killed, the accused were taken to Melbourne where they were tried. After just three minutes' deliberation by the jury Ptolemy and Booby were found guilty while their accomplice, Bullet-Eye, was acquitted. The two convicted men, scared, in tears and perhaps not totally understanding what was happening to them, were hanged a month later. Bullet-Eye was made to watch. A report from the day suggested they should be hanged at the place of the murder so as to send a direct message to others of similar mind. Although that was not carried out, the message got through anyway. A young white shepherd was the next person killed by the Aborigines; he was found with a knotted rope around his neck.

After a few days pottering around on the river at Swan Hill I set off again, planning to stop about 30 kilometres downstream.

Heading towards Nyah, I had to wait for the Speewa Ferry to make its way across the river. The ferry is only the second in Victoria, although there are still twelve more operating in South Australia. In operation since 1913, the ferry trip saves passengers about 25 kilometres of travel between Speewa Island and Swan Hill.

There were once a number of swamps around the Nyah area. Regular flooding would have been caused by the existence at the time of a natural weir formed from river debris and snags on a bend near a place once known as Touchabel. Snagging operations removed the obstruction, causing the swamps to dry up and the local Watti Watti people to lose a valuable food source.

Walking through the Vinifera Forest, where some of the swamps once were, my thoughts were of the time when Aborigines hunted and fished here, feasting on mussels, swans and magpie geese. They'd tie cumbungi roots together and steam them in middens before chewing the nourishment out and keeping the fibre to manufacture thread, headbands and twine. They'd play games such as 'wotchwie', in which a wooden device with a long tail was thrown between people, and a ball game with a stuffed possum skin in which the entire tribe— both men and women—would take part. Then there was a form of skipping using a nine-metre long rope made from cumbungi twine, and spear-throwing at a disc of bark rolled along the ground. In all their games, trying too hard to win was considered bad manners.

At the other end of the forest was a small plaque, a monument to Jo Takasuka. A Japanese man credited with growing the first commercial rice in Australia, Jo came to the country in 1905 and was granted 200 acres of land, which he laid out for his rice crop. A levee bank still forms part of the road into the forest. Why Jo would choose to come here was anyone's guess. Why he wanted to grow rice was a bit easier to understand.

Late in the day, just along from the bollard depicting Pearl Wallace that stood in the Nyah Forest close to the spot the *Kookaburra* had sunk, I pitched the tent where, with my brothers and father, I had camped and fished many times over the years, and where the Aboriginal presence was quite evident.

There were over a hundred middens and burial sites in the forest as well as a few ring trees. These marked different tribal lands and had their branches tied down with bark or sinews until they grew into each other over a number of years. Visiting tribes who saw one of these trees had to wait and identify themselves before being invited onto the lands.

A search for the place where I had been invited to be part of an Aboriginal reburial many years before was unsuccessful, but my memories of the simple, moving ceremony, when the remains of six members of the Watti Watti clan were laid back in the soil from whence they came, were clear. The centuries-old remains of an old man, two women and a man aged in their thirties, and two children had been exhumed in 1978 for studies. After much discussion they had been given back to their descendants so they could be returned to rest in their spiritual home.

The burial site, as well as those present, was cleansed of bad spirits by the smoke from a small fire of eucalyptus leaves lit by women. The ceremonial leader placed the bones on a bed of leaves in the graves. The skull and head bones were placed facing the east so the spirits could see the sun rise, while the other bones were laid as close as they could get to the shape of the body. The bones were then covered by layers of bark and sticks to prevent them being dug up by animals.

As the profoundly moving ceremony ended, and being the only white person there, it was time to leave. The Aboriginal people set up camps. As one told me, 'We'll stay with the old people tonight; we'll sit here while they reconnect with their land.' As I left, the women were singing their spirits home in their traditional language.

After Nyah, the Murray confirmed its reputation as being the most winding river in the world. It curled around and around and was full of snags. Distances on the river were almost three times those by road, even though in some places the river had become straighter after cutting through some of the bends. The river's contortions took me past the same house four times and at Gallows Bend it almost cut back on itself. In another few hundred years, perhaps, there would be another anabranch, another island. And even though at the moment the river was flush with rains, would it still be flowing then? Would it have dried up, or become a rotten mess of salt, dead trees and poisonous algae? Gallows Bend seemed an ideal place to reflect on the possibility.

Rain had made it easier to negotiate the river but even though the bottom wasn't visible, its presence was always apparent. As I powered under the Tooleybuc Bridge towards Goodnight, the occasional scrape of a snag under the boat told me so.

A small settlement close to the river bank, Goodnight was so named thanks to a farm worker who would camp near the bend and call out 'goodnight' to those on the passing steamers, no matter what time of day.

Around Goodnight the river was a mess of tangled snags, making it almost impassable in low water and very dangerous even in high water. This was a place where the river was at its most obstinate, when, if it was in the mood, it could stop anyone using it at all. When it let everyone know who was in charge. When it played with those who took it for granted.

The biggest and most infamous hazard was the 'Bitch and Pups', a series of rocks and muddy islands that, for over a hundred years, caused many a boat grief. There were many stories about how the reef was named but the most common was that the biggest of the islands is the Bitch and two of the smaller ones are the Pups.

In 1964, when the *Oscar W* towed the *Gem* to Swan Hill, the boats were stranded there for eight months. When they were at last able to move, Paddy Hogg was joined onboard by his wife, Pearl Wallace. At one stage Pearl was handed a bunch of lilac by an old lady who had done the same thing to the crew of the *Gem* on its maiden voyage.

Approaching the Bitch and Pups my carefree attitude dissipated and, sensibly, I decided to go no further. Even though the river had been kind to me for a long while now, my navigation skills were not the best and if I tempted it too much the river might see me stuck or, worse, sunk. Only part of the reef was visible but, like icebergs, I knew what was underneath.

So out came the boat and we headed for the junction of the Wakool, the river that had left the Edward, which in turn had left the Murray. All three rivers had now joined again in the mother river, having given and gathered waters from across New South Wales. This was also close to Poon Boon station, where Francis Cadell loaded the first bale of wool for transportation to Goolwa onto the *Lady Augusta* in September 1853.

I'd come to the Wakool junction a few times over the years trying to catch fish, as usual without much luck. This time it would be different. With a good river, a pleasant day and a couple of nice spots with running water my optimism was high—even though my worms were looking decidedly thin and dry. This was a place where the Cobb and Co coaches had stopped and where a professional fisherman called Scotty would load the many cod he caught into the coach bound for Swan Hill. In the heat of summer he would lay a blanket of gum leaves across the fish to keep them cool and to stop them going off. Scotty would have been a handy source of advice, as whatever fish he had left in the river certainly were not about to visit my line. An hour passed without so much as a nibble. Understanding there would be no catches of even a single fish, and as it was about 40 kilometres on the river but only half that by road, I drove to Boundary Bend just downstream from the Murrumbidgee junction.

On a long sweeping double curve with immense sandbars on either side, Boundary Bend was named because it was where two properties originally had their boundaries. Across from the river was a shop, which doubled as the petrol station and caravan park office as well as a Medicare office, post office and newsagency. Shelves were stacked with fishing gear for sale—although the bait didn't look any better than mine—and a table piled with brochures and flyers from many and varying organisations stood in the corner.

The biggest pile of flyers was made up of the Truckies Evangelist Newsletter, which told truck drivers how they could pass the time in their cabins by praying, how the Lord guided them and their trucks, and where church services were held on their routes.

After jealously studying the pictures of caravan park visitors with their huge cod, I put the boat back in the water and headed upstream to see where Sturt had arrived in 1830—the Murrumbidgee junction. It only took half an hour to reach the junction that, in a direct line must have only been a couple of kilometres from the highway.

The myth of a great inland sea had been perpetuated for years, especially after the Blue Mountains were crossed and many westward-flowing rivers were found. Joseph Banks, the botanist on Captain Cook's voyages, even said: 'It is impossible to concede that such a large body of land, as large as all Europe, does not produce vast rivers, capable of being navigated into the heart of the interior.'

Charles Sturt was also a believer, to the point of taking a few whaleboats with him on his explorations into central Australia even after he had discovered the Murray. Earlier, Sturt had led an expedition along the Macquarie River and had come to what he thought was an important watercourse, even though it was badly affected by drought. He named the river the Darling after the governor who authorised the trip, and followed it for a few days before turning back. A year later Sturt was sent down the Lachlan River to the Murrumbidgee to solve what was termed the 'riddle of the rivers'. At Maude, near the spot where the Lachlan meets the Murrumbidgee, sections of a whaleboat Sturt and his men had carted all the way from Sydney were assembled, together with another smaller skiff built by a carpenter on the riverbank. On 7 January 1830, Sturt, assisted by George Macleay and accompanied by a crew of six, began his voyage. Two days later the skiff struck a snag and sank and two days were spent recovering the stores that sank with it.

On 14 January, when he reached the junction of the Murray, Sturt wrote that he was 'launched into a broad and noble river, flowing east to west.' He named the river after Sir George Murray, the Colonial Secretary. Little did he know that Hume and Hovell, up the other end, had already named the river. With some assistance from sails, Sturt's men then rowed their whaleboat down the Murray to reach Goolwa before turning it around and rowing all the way back. Although they didn't discover a sea, in some ways the explorers were on the right track; a great inland sea did exist once—they were just a few million years too late.

Sturt was right; the Murray was broad and, despite its problems, it was still noble. It was also peaceful once the boat's motor had stopped. Sitting on the bank directly opposite the Murrumbidgee as it stealthily joined the 'broad and noble river', a pelican waiting patiently on a fallen tree looked at me briefly, then turned his gaze back to the water. Two kangaroos bounded down to the water's edge on the other side before raising their heads and leaping away. Bird songs echoed through the trees; each with a different voice, each in turn. Trees, some of which must have seen both Sturt and I, stood silent guard over the water. Others, their burls and dead branches still visible, lay asleep in the muddy yet tranquil water.

On the road into Robinvale a huge mobile sign warned of the dangers of speeding in four languages—English and three others that looked Arabic. Many nationalities were represented in Robinvale's population, most of them being farm workers. While I was trying to start the boat motor at the caravan park, a couple of locals told me about a chap who had worked out a way to run the engine on his boat with cooking oil. Apparently he used the leftover canola oil from the local fish and chip shop. As the engine spluttered into life I asked where he was and, unhelpfully, they said he wasn't around for a week or so. They also said the town had a few problems with the ethnic divide but nothing that couldn't be fixed with a few simple rules. I didn't ask what the rules or the problems were, instead I took off under the bridge. Or, actually, the bridge and a half.

The old wooden bridge was being replaced; while it had served its purpose faithfully, it was badly in need of a rest. The replacement was a concrete monstrosity that rose high above the surrounding area in sections from both sides. A black crane that looked like a gigantic stick insect rose from its fixed position on a pontoon in the river and swung huge buckets of concrete out to the workers. With the width of the river and the quiet dignity of the old bridge it all looked out of place, but not out of time. The locals had wanted the new bridge for years, though there was a touch of sadness about losing the old one.

After taking a sharp turn south at Robinvale, the Murray headed for Euston in New South Wales. Established by Edmund Morey in 1846 Euston was the elder of the two towns, which were only a few kilometres apart. The following year, John Grant obtained 19 000 acres at what was then known as Bumbang, after a large island in the river which was home to the Yitha-Yitha people. He later sold to Herbert Cuttle, who settled on what would become Robinvale's town site in 1916. When the railway arrived in 1924, plans were made for a bridge and work on the Euston Weir began. Cuttle then decided to sell part of his land and a special train from Melbourne was organised so that prospective buyers could attend the auction. The town that was established was named after Cuttle's son, Robin, an airman who was killed over France in World War I. After World War II, Robinvale became a soldier settlement district with blocks being set up with grapevines and citrus trees.

Robinvale is the sister city of the northern French town of Villers-Bretonneux. The two places are much the same size and Australian regiments who fought to liberate the French town in the Great War were mainly from Victoria, many of them from the Robinvale district. The quote *N'oublions jamais l'Australie* (Let us never forget Australia) appears in the classrooms of the school of Villers–Bretonneux, which was rebuilt after the war with money raised by donations from Victoria. A plaque at the school reads:

> *This school building is the gift of the schoolchildren of Victoria, Australia to the children of Villers-Bretonneux, as a proof of their love and goodwill towards France. Twelve hundred Australian soldiers, the fathers and brothers of these children, gave their lives in the heroic recapture of this town from the invader on 24 April 1918 and are buried near this spot. May the memory of great sacrifices in a common cause keep France and Australia together forever in bonds of friendship and mutual esteem.*

The sun spread across the river at Euston, rising above the trees on the bank and spearing through the mist that lifted almost imperceptibly until it was finally gone. A mass of flapping wings disturbed the sheen of the water as a pair of ducks flew off and then landed a few metres away. A magpie warbled above me, peering down from the lowest branch of the venerable red gum at the man emerging from inside the *Coorong Wanderer*, the boat tied to the red gum's trunk.

Kendall Jones, a rotund figure, wore shorts, a stained T-shirt and nothing on his feet. He grinned a good morning and invited me on board. He and his wife, who introduced herself as 'cook' but was also known as Roma, lived in Goolwa and had spent their life on or near the river.

An excavator for many years, one of Kendall's contracts had involved replacing the beacon pylons in Lake Alexandrina. Part of the deal was being able to salvage the old pylons; the tops were rotten, but underneath the water they were in perfect condition, even after almost sixty years. In Kendall's mind at the time was his perfect boat, so he asked a friend to sketch his thoughts, which soon became a simple drawing of the boat's outline. Kendall then turned it into reality. The red gum pylons formed a large part of his plans. He wanted to use the wood in the boat—and, after five years of drying it out, he did. While Kendall built the metal parts, the wood was used by a mate to build tables, chairs, window surrounds, even the dashboard where all the boat's gauges were. It was a piece of art. In the main bedroom there was even a four-poster bed carved out of red gum. After four years the *Coorong Wanderer* was launched and the couple could fulfil their dream of travelling the river system.

'We're both from the Murray and, once you've got a connection to it, well, you know,' said Roma, 'we just needed to see all of it, or at least as much as we could.'

They decided they would like to see where all the South Australian water came from and why all the rubbish washed down to them. Roma remembered swimming in the river as a girl and seeing almost to the bottom. But now, her voice trailed off as she shrugged her shoulders. Overall, she said, they'd found that the river was everything they expected, 'the good and the bad'.

Kendall was, as Roma put it, supposedly retired, but he was constantly approached with offers of work. One of his more challenging tasks was to transport a couple of huge pontoons up the river from Goolwa to Wentworth, a distance of some 830 kilometres. The pontoons would then have cranes placed on them to perform work on the lock and weir.

The first pontoon was picked up at Goolwa and taken across Lake Alexandrina, while the other was hooked on at Lyrup in the Riverland. A caravan and a ute were secured on board and, powered by an ex-army diesel motor lashed to the rear of the pontoons, the journey began.

'Took us twenty-one days,' said Kendall. 'The contraption was so long that going round bends was really hairy. Plenty of times we'd be almost hitting one bank and touching the other as we went round.'

Before I left them, Kendall took me on a tour of the *Coorong Wanderer*. The open-air spa and his fishing gear and the small boat strapped to the stern were infinitely more elaborate then my tinnie.

If it wasn't for the sign it would have been easy to miss Wemen as there wasn't much there, just a shop that doubled as a service station with a couple of sheds alongside. What wasn't on show was the incredible diversity of produce grown in the district. All along the river I had seen a bounty of products grown with its water. Here, though, there was a slight difference. Wemen was on the edge of a desert which the river cut through. For a few kilometres either side of the river the land appeared like an oasis, but beyond that was dry barren mallee soil where crops grew only if it rained, which wasn't very often.

Near the river you could grow almost anything. At Wemen, apart from the usual plantings of grapes, there were olives, almonds, citrus and a huge farm that grew carrots by the paddock full; hundreds and hundreds of acres of carrots. Huge semitrailer loads of carrots were sent to Melbourne and Sydney each day. It was said the owner had a special dam fenced off that he'd stocked with fish for his own pleasure. As the river turned west again so did I, into the Hattah-Kulkyne National Park.

At the information centre a clearly knowledgeable man was studying the park. Ben, a naturalist, had a professorial look and was only too pleased to share his understanding of the surrounds. He explained that the seventeen lakes in the park were joined and fed by Chalka Creek, an anabranch that funnelled the water in when the Murray flooded, which was very seldom. The last time it happened the flood was only small; the last good flood when everything was filled was in 1996. The lakes had been dry many times, in fact if there was no water for two years most tended to dry out. Environmental flows every now and again gave some respite, said Ben, but it was never enough. Historically the lakes filled more often than they once did but they also emptied more often and stayed empty for much longer. A regulator on the creek originally put in to provide water for steam trains helped to a certain degree, but basically the lakes were left to nature.

Outside Ben pointed beyond a cluster of box trees. 'Away from the river vegetation is a lot different. You'll get different plants and flowers in the sand dunes, a small ecosystem of its own almost.'

He said that the natural system had not changed greatly over the years but the changes in the river were causing problems for the park. 'The black box and red gums are in danger. If regular flooding doesn't occur then these trees will die.'

White man had settled here in the 1840s, when the Jari Jari tribe occupied the land. Translated the name meant 'no', and apparently the tribe were given the name because of the frequent use of the word. It was said they came to the area because too many others were living on the river and there was plenty of space this short distance inland.

Early European settlers had thought only a few Aborigines would occupy this place, and that they would only come for hunting and gathering excursions, that it was inhospitable and too dry. There was always plenty of food—kangaroos, emus and so on—but water was a concern. However, if you knew where to look, then it wasn't at all as arid as those settlers imagined.

113

Aborigines used soaks, small indents in the ground where surface water ran off and accumulated. Dew on leaves was another obvious way of collecting water. Belah trees had partly hollowed wood in the junction of their branches and, by dipping a spear with dry grass into the hole they'd get the rain-water that had gathered there. Some of the roots from mallee trees also held water. These would be cut into lengths and stood upright in a hollowed-out burl or burnt trunk with the end that had been furthest from the trunk at the top. Up to a litre of water would eke out in half an hour.

Water would be kept in bags made from the skins of possums or kangaroos. These skins would be peeled inside out and the leg and arm holes tied with sinews or pieces of stringy-bark. The fur would be left on so the water's impurities would become caught in it. When the water was used, most of the dirt gathered with it had gone. Occasionally the Aborigines would walk to the river to collect water in those rudimentary containers.

In the sandhills I walked through the trees Ben had described then, emerging from the scrub, I sat and listened to the plaintive cry of a strange bird. Walking a bit further, I came across a grave surrounded by a small weather-beaten wooden post and rail. James Mahon—drowned in Chalka Creek—63 years—21.12.1923—RIP.

James Mahon lay at the foot of a sandhill looking towards the creek, now dry, in which he had drowned. If anybody was resting in peace, it was James.

Shortly after leaving the park the road took me through the small hamlet of Colignan, and a short distance down the road I came upon Nangiloc. In the store I asked how the names came about. A customer reckoned that he didn't know and the man who served him said the same. The bloke helping himself to petrol at the bowser said that many years ago, after a conflict, someone had moved from one of the places to the other and decided to call the place he settled the name of the original place spelt backwards. Or was it the other way around? Whatever was true and whichever was the original town didn't matter; either version was impressive.

Not too far away, out in the mallee country, was Nowingi, the place where the Victorian government planned to locate a toxic waste dump. Local people were disconcerted and annoyed, some outrightly defiant. Bumper stickers with 'No Toxic Waste' appeared on many cars and trucks. Posters conveying the same message were on trees, fences and attached to buildings. The locals called their region 'Victoria's food bowl' and were worried not only about leakage but about their reputation around the world. Food grown next to toxic waste dumps would not be easily sold in some countries. Then, of course, there was the Murray. If anything managed to find its way into the water then it wouldn't be only this area that would suffer. The government dismissed all their concerns; the people were assured there would be no problems. But as one local said, 'If there's no problem and it's so safe, why bother spending all the money transporting it 500 kilometres up here? Keep it in Melbourne.'

Red Cliffs, almost a suburb of Mildura, was in the middle of the section of the Murray known as the Mallee Trench, where the river cut through the soft sandy ground with ease. Red Cliffs was also the first place on the river where I had seen actual cliffs. There had been places with red dunes and banks that were tall, but no cliffs. One side of the river was flat but the other rose 70 metres above it, a mountain around which the river had traced its path. From the flat side of the river the cliffs looked majestic. From the top of them the flat side looked ordinary. Between them the river crawled along, not caring too much about either.

Red Cliffs was the home of Big Lizzie. Standing proudly under a tin-roofed display centre in the main street this steel curiosity was a reminder of the days when necessity and imagination were indeed the mother of invention. Big Lizzie was built in 1919 by Frank Bottrill, a Melbourne inventor who wanted to make a machine that would not fall prey to the huge sand dunes in this part of the country. A year or so earlier, when taking a steam traction engine to Broken Hill to replace the camel trains, Bottrill had become hopelessly bogged. Upon returning to Melbourne he decided to invent the 'unboggable' wheel. He attached lengths of wood to a wheel replicating the way timber is placed under a machine so as to make its path over sand quite easy. These wheels became the foundation of Big Lizzie.

Bottrill set out for Broken Hill on Big Lizzie along with a huge trailer of similar size, expecting to complete the journey in nine months. Two years later, after dropping through a couple of bridges and being forced by local councils to travel only on roads, he arrived in Mildura. Big Lizzie was finally put to work clearing land around Red Cliffs for what was to be the biggest soldier settlement in Australia.

The only one in the world, Big Lizzie was successful to a degree, although she could only move at two kilometres per hour and had a turning circle of some 70 metres that required eighty turns of the huge steering wheel. Still, though she might have looked gawky, she played her part in the district's evolution. A nursery where more than a million vine cuttings were grown was established, after which seven hundred diggers arrived.

The Southern Hemisphere's largest pumping station was built and supplied water through channels to the vines and citrus trees planted in the land that Big Lizzie had helped clear.

Late spring

Mildura to Loxton

After the blossoms on the stone-fruit trees have turned to leaves and the vines have sprouted even further along the way to fruit, and before the sun becomes almost unbearably hot, there is no better place to be than along the Murray in these parts.

The spring winds had almost gone when I set out again. The football season had finished and cricket was on the way. The world was still in a state of angst—or at least those who controlled it were. It seemed to me that if you had money then there was nothing to worry about, but reading what politicians had to say made me want to stay on the river. There I'd be away from the new IR laws, away from the terrorists who supposedly might turn up at any given moment, and away from the constant, nauseating drone of the government explaining how well they were looking after us. I'd also be away from all those of the opposite persuasion who thought that the answer to everything was to slander everything the government did. The river was a great option and while on it the world was irrelevant.

Summer had shown itself a few times, with the occasional day reaching the thirties and the nights staying warm. The Slow River seems to flow even slower during these times, its tranquillity projecting calmness across everything, extending even to blokes in tinnies who felt just like the river. I wanted to be slow, to enjoy the surrounds and loll about doing nothing, to watch others doing the same. If someone came along who actually worked, I wanted to watch them watching me jealously. I wanted to watch the slow methodical beats of a pelican's wings and count the cries of the river gulls. To see if I could catch the leaves on the top of the gums as they moved when the slight breeze wafted through them. And as the sun rose and fell to see the shadows on the water spread like invaders on the day.

I slipped the tinnie into the river just above Psyche Bend and headed sedately downstream towards Mildura's city centre. It was early Sunday morning and, even without calendars or clocks or papers or radios, I'd always know the special feeling of Sunday. There is something ethereal that gives Sunday a distinct atmosphere; this Sunday particularly so with the sun and the water and the stillness of the world.

It was hard to imagine what Mildura would have been like if the Chaffey brothers hadn't come here. In 1884, during the years of almost ceaseless droughts, Alfred Deakin (who was later to become Prime Minister) was chairman of the Victorian government's inquiry into irrigation and water supply. On a trip to Canada to examine their watering systems he met the Chaffey brothers, George and William. They were duly offered 100 000 hectares of land to come and set up an irrigation settlement, utilising the water of the Murray.

George Chaffey came to the country and selected Mildura as his preferred site but there was significant resistance to giving 'these foreigners' crown land. As the controversy raged, and the land was thrown open to public tender—but no one else was interested and no other offers were forthcoming. In the meantime, the South Australians slipped in and offered the Chaffeys land at Renmark, which they duly accepted. In 1887 Renmark became the first irrigation settlement on the river. But by 1890 the Chaffeys were back in Mildura. Their project was publicised worldwide and the area soon was inundated with migrants.

At Pysche Bend the Chaffeys used the paddle-steamer *Jane Eliza* as a pump station for their first efforts before their own pumps were built. The new pumps were part of the largest irrigation plant in the world and served the district for seventy years until replaced by new electrical units.

Seemingly endless rows of vines disappeared into the distance as I puttered along enjoying the morning. In the midst of many vineyards were large brick mansions, and every now and then a winery appeared with houseboats tied up in front. As the clock ticked towards midmorning, an array of watercraft joined me on the water, all enjoying Sunday.

Mildura had grown significantly in recent years. In some places the change was obvious. On many farms, alongside the new brick houses stood old weatherboard places, paint dried and stripping off, verandah poles leaning awkwardly. A few had tractors parked in the old carports. These were the homes of the original farmers, who had battled the land and whom the river had smiled upon with her riches; those who had turned the hard times into the successes they now enjoyed.

Sundays are usually a day of rest but here there was work to be done. The burble of the machinery in the vineyards and citrus orchards was joined by the noise of the traffic in the city. The couple who waved at me from a grassy bank were clearly of

Italian extraction but, just as clearly, were not working. Tony had a heavily stubbled face where his sideburns disappeared into whiskers and he wore a battered towelling hat. A third-generation Australian, he remained proud of his heritage. Connie, his wife, had lived in the area all her life as well. They had been married for thirty years.

'Our place is over there, away from the river,' Tony said, sweeping his arms around. 'A good place that my grandparents and my parents worked hard for and then gave to us.'

Tony and Connie had been spending time in this spot for years. 'We walk down here a lot in the afternoon and on Sundays after church and just sit and look at the river. We think about how lucky we are.'

Tony remembered how, in the old days, local families worked together at pruning time and at harvest. 'Everyone helped each other, still happens some places but in others it's changed.'

Tony said he supported the new wave of immigration but worried about the way newcomers were received. He shrugged his shoulders and spread his hands wide. 'We know what it's like—we went through it in the fifties and sixties,' he said. 'Anyway, we're lucky, we have the best of both countries.'

Tony said that he had made friends from everywhere, especially during the years when they had pickers from all over the world. These days there were not so many pickers; machines have taken their place. Where once there were hundreds of workers on farms, now machines creep along between the vines like giant mechanical monsters and prune and pick and spray without the need for men and women. Clusters of old, battered caravans parked near machinery sheds indicated there were still farmers who used itinerant labour, but they were becoming fewer.

On each side of the river, grand houses were a testament to the area's wealth. On one side there were grass banks down to the water's edge with small jetties, while on the side with cliffs elaborate walkways led from the houses down to similar jetties.

On the bank near the Mildura bridge a circus tent was being erected. An elephant was chained nearby and a few horses grazed in a fenced-off area. Collections of river gulls landed near them, scrutinised the ground and flew away. Inquisitive children inspected the animals and the huge tent, while other less interested couples lay on the grass and watched the river and its traffic go by.

I loaded the boat near Lock 11, the next downstream from Lock 15 at Euston. (The three in between had never been built.) Lock 11 was the only spot on the river where the weir and the lock were separated. A tranquil, grassy island that was open to the public when there were no boats in the lock was always open to pelicans. While estimating the difference in river height between the two sides of the lock I watched a lone pelican paddling around and wondered whether the birds could be trained to work for fishermen who couldn't catch anything. Given my own marked lack of success as a fisherman, a pet pelican would be ideal. He could ride with me in my tinnie and catch fish for me while I sat back and watched him, generously feeding him the occasional smaller one.

Back from the lock, along the riverfront, paddle-steamers were moored—the *Melbourne*, the *Rothbury*, the *Wandoo*. Another was the *Avoca*, which housed a restaurant owned by Stefano de Pieri, who had been named an official 'Murray River Ambassador', meaning he was dedicated to promoting everything about the river.

Born in Treviso near Venice, Stefano came to Australia in 1974, graduating in politics and Italian from Melbourne

University. He had always dabbled in food, but took a job in the public service before coming to Mildura in 1991. Stefano's passion for food and for the Murray River has been obvious for years. His television program *Gondola on the Murray* was a huge success for the ABC and his world-famous restaurant in Mildura's Grand Hotel was a continual award winner.

As well as operating his land-based restaurant, Stefano spent some time during the week cooking lunches aboard the Avoca Riverfront Café. On Sundays the paddle-steamer travelled up the river with his famous 'long table lunch'. As it was Sunday I accepted the invitation to join them. We left shortly after noon.

The *Avoca* was a cargo vessel in the 1870s, then spent time underwater during the 1920s before being resurrected and becoming a popular nightspot in the 1970s. With Stefano's input— together with his friends, the Chalmers family—the boat had become a relaxing, informal riverfront café ready for the next hundred years.

Upstairs, in front of the glassed-in walls designed to protect us from any winds, enthusiastic diners of all ages soon filled the seats while Stefano fussed around, making sure his cooking apparatus was in proper order and all the ingredients he needed were close at hand.

My seat was next to a visiting wine writer, Tim White. Tim had been in Mildura judging the Alternate Varieties Wine Show and had an immense knowledge of wine that he was more than willing to share. An Englishman by birth, Tim had fallen for Australia and Australian wines. He loved the river and had a great relationship with Stefano, having visited the region many times to write about Sunraysia's wine and food. Not a wine snob but rather a wine enthusiast, Tim chose the wine and I drank it with him. We made a good team, I thought.

As the paddles took us away from the mooring with their rhythmic beat, Stefano was up and down the stairs while people gathered round his cooking table, taking photographs of him at work. The breeze had picked up a touch but it was still a magnificent day, the sun shining on the willows and the gum trees, some people chattering excitedly while others simply gazed in silence at the unfolding life on the river.

As small, brown bready morsels with tasty green topping were served as nibbles to accompany the wine, Tim told me about one of his pet hates, the waste of water. 'You've got this amazing river system and it is absolutely abused. I find it incredible, the lack of respect for the river.'

Tim thought that we should take notice of the ways of the original inhabitants of the land and we'd learn a bit. Tim also considered that, although it might sound simplistic, we were still using irrigation practices more suitable to European countries, where there's almost unlimited rainfall. 'But out here?' he asked. 'In this country? We suck everything out of the river and assume that it's always going to be there.'

He'd flown in to Adelaide once and seen the dredges trying to keep the Murray mouth open while massive clattering sprinklers at the airport were watering lawns that no one would ever sit on, where no would ever play, and at which no one would ever look twice.

So why did an English-born wine writer who lives in Melbourne care about that?

'Because this country is now my home and it's just wrong. I'd feel the same no matter where I lived.' There will be, said Tim, unnecessary damage foisted on future generations because our generations don't care enough.

The entrée—a risotto of fresh Murray River yabbies and crayfish—was accompanied by another bottle of Tim's choice, which went down extremely well. As I wiped the excess from the corners of my mouth as delicately as possible, Tim told me that now he had seen some of the places affected by drought and the effects of salt, it had made him understand more about it. In some parts of the river he had a feeling of it dying by 'a thousand cuts', while in other places it felt almost like being in a cemetery.

Just outside Mildura are a number of salt evaporation basins where salt is pumped after being removed from the river. Each day over 1000 tonnes of salt are pumped into these places and one, the Morquong Basin, has more than a million tonnes of salt lying on the ground. Even though the salt is being harvested and becoming a product in demand all over the world, it is still quite astounding to think it all comes from the Murray River.

In the absence of a decent Murray cod, the main course was a salmon cooked inside a big loaf of bread. (It actually had a much more sophisticated name, but that was what it looked like to me.) Stefano—who called the dish by its proper name—prepared it in front of those wanting advice, which he gave freely. After we disposed of another exquisite drop I wandered out onto the prow and watched the captain steer us towards a forest of dead trees where two tinnies were anchored. One had a solitary occupant while the other, much lower in the water, held six blokes in blue singlets, their hands gripping stubbies. Noticeably, there were no obvious signs of fish in either boat. I wouldn't have swapped places anyway.

Blowing her whistle, the *Avoca* lurched around and we headed back. Stefano came over to make sure everything was going well, which we assured him it was. He then wandered along the table, answering questions as he had when he was preparing the meal, making everybody feel his attention was on them—not because he had to, but because he wanted to.

We then consumed a tasty dessert and agreed that it was certainly a refined way to spend a Sunday afternoon.

When we pulled in to the wharf and the passengers had all departed, and when Tim and I had finally, after a worthy battle, finished the requisite amount of bottles, Stefano and I sat on the deck outside.

As a young man, he had lived near the Sile River that ran near his village of Casier. Stefano thought the Sile and the Murray had a connection because they were both rivers, and 'the rivers are different and yet the same'. 'Very different,' he said. 'The Sile had fast clear water, this is slow and windy and brown, but there is still something similar about them.'

Stefano's father didn't have a very strong connection to the river and didn't go there much; he was more a lover of the sea. His uncle was the fisherman of the family. 'He was always down there fishing in the river and would come back with pike and eels and tenches hanging from his bike's handlebars.'

In Stefano's opinion, there is something different about river people. While it is good to have a connection with nature anywhere, one with the river is extra-special. 'I may be imagining it, but river people seem to have another dimension,' he said. 'I'm not sure what it is about these men or women who love the boats or the water, but you can sense something, it's intuitive.'

We talked about migrants who came to the river; about his friends and mine. About the way it has had a multicultural population since the beginning of navigation.

'Chinese cooks, Afghans, Germans,' he said. 'It's been that way forever with all the adventurers, pioneers, but it's even more prevalent here and further downstream.'

Although living in Mildura has given Stefano immense commercial success, in great part due to the river, it has also given him spirituality, made him a different person, more at peace with himself and his life. He finds what the American author Richard Florida said to be true: that the economic development of a city is related to the creativity found there; that creative places are more successful and are better places in which to live. 'We have tremendous creativity here—writers, chefs, winemakers, all of it works together and none can work at its best without the other.'

But nowhere is perfect, Stefano added. Every day the lawns at the front of the *Avoca*'s mooring, as well as those further along, are used by people eating fast food, and every day their litter is left around. 'A lot of it goes into the river and, apart from that, each morning I spend half an hour picking up rubbish.' Stefano had paid for two pollution interceptors in the river near the *Avoca*, and when it rains he collects 10 or 12 tonnes of rubbish, cans, butts, wrappers, bottles and the like. 'It makes me so angry how can people do that,' he said. 'They get their benefits from the river and then do that to it.'

Stefano said that, at times, he despairs for the river and for the world; that his hopes for them both are the same; that something substantial will be done by governments. He is doing his part by conducting a campaign to save the red gums along the river. 'Many of these beautiful, majestic trees in the forest are being sacrificed to loggers and end up as woodchips. We can't simply go on doing this; we can't.'

Did he think the river had a soul?

Stefano savoured his words. 'Ah, the big brown god. Yes, I think it has. I'd like to think it has. Otherwise, why do we feel like this?'

After spending the night downstream from Mildura, away from any lights, away from any human contact, I was on the river before dawn after being woken by two kookaburras and a magpie arguing in the trees. The previous evening a swarm of sulphur-crested cockatoos had flown in an indeterminate mess across the pinks and blues of the fading sun, their white bodies stark against the sky. Their voices were in full cry, a cacophony of noise. Listening closely I had picked out different sounds, one finishing as another started. A soprano beginning her call, a low baritone ending his. There was no background noise, just the silence sliced up in different tones, like listening to a symphony orchestra when you hear different instruments at different times. The birds circled above me three times, making sure every nuance, every octave was apparent in a feathered stereophonic concert.

The droning motor soon replaced the sounds of the kookaburras, the magpie and all the other birds that had been listening to the start of another day. Voltaire was right when he said that animals have advantages over humans. They never hear the clock strike, they die without any idea of death, they have no religious overseers and their last moments are not clouded by ceremonies over which they have no control. Maybe that's not exactly what he said, but the birds and I knew what he meant.

My idea was to take the tinnie the 50 river kilometres to Wentworth, approaching the junction with the Darling River in much the same way as Sturt had. Pulling up at a sandbar just past Cowanna Bend, I wondered if this was where Sturt had found trouble with the locals.

A few days before he arrived in Wentworth, a few Aborigines had come into his camp after the tents were pitched. Sturt pacified them, and, with the help of his second in command George Macleay, a red-headed Scotsman, made friends with the chief. A couple of days later a mob of about six hundred appeared on a sandbar dressed in warpaint, thinking, perhaps, that he was some sort of spirit coming down the river in a small boat with a sail. Sturt kept well clear of them but eventually, worried about an attack, raised his gun and was about to fire when a figure ran out of the bush and swam across the river. The Aborigines left quietly and later Sturt discovered that the peace-maker was the chief whom he had befriended earlier.

Could this have been the place? Probably not, but then the sandbars hadn't changed much since that time. Or even before that time. It was similar to the feeling I'd had when walking into King's College in Cambridge and looking at the stone doorstep that was bowed in the middle from feet wearing it out over the centuries. There my imagination conjured up all the different people who had walked on the stone. Here there was only Sturt and the Aborigines. With my back against a tree and my fingers in the sand, I thought about those before me who had listened to the birds; who had stood here or sat in the sand, and watched this body of water pass them by.

The Darling joined the Murray just before Lock 10, slipping alongside, almost flowing in the same direction. Sturt knew the river he'd come across was the Darling and was pleased that he'd found it again. He had every right to feel that way as his journey in the whaleboat had caused him and his party a number of problems. The crew rowed a short distance upstream to make sure he was right, then, 'I directed the Union Jack to be hoisted and, giving way to our satisfaction, we all stood up in the boat and gave three distinct cheers.'

The Darling flowed a lot more quickly when Sturt was visiting than it did now, nearly as quickly as the Murray. Sturt noted that 'the strength of the currents must be nearly equal since there was a distinct line between their respective waters, as if a thin channel separated them. The one half of the channel contained the turbid waters of the northern stream, the other still preserved the original transparency.'

Sturt had seen what river men would see later: the colour of the Darling water. At its worst there was a distinct difference between the water spreading across the junction of the two rivers: the clay from the Darling and the red sand of the Murray.

Carmel Chapman, of the Wentworth Visitor Information Centre, had an obvious and intense passion for the area. A Darling River advocate, Carmel explained why the water was a different colour.

'Nature sends clay soil down the river,' she said. 'It doesn't send down red sand because we already have that. We have become the delta of the Darling.'

Carmel said that if the Murray was supposed to be in danger then the Darling was in absolute peril. It had very little flow, poisonous blue-green algae was prevalent when the river stopped, and the amount of water taken out by cotton farms was astronomical. One of them had a water right that was more than half the total of all water rights in South Australia. 'Twenty-five rivers flow into the Darling,' Carmel informed me. 'So it is not only the amount of water they take out, it's the chemicals and fertilisers that pollute what there is left.' 'To save both rivers,' she continued, 'we need an appreciation of the whole system from up in Queensland down to here. The Murray from here on is nothing without the Darling.'

The Darling had as many stories about riverboats as did the Murray. There were ports at Wilcannia, Bourke and Menindee as well as many more further upstream. Distances across land were so great towards Queensland and in the outback of New South Wales that the Darling was ideal for transport, even if the flows were so fragile there were often long periods when boats were stranded. Before the advent of paddle-boats, the wool clip could be left on remote stations for two years or more because there weren't enough bullock wagons to take them the long distances to Melbourne or Sydney. When the steamers started their runs up the Darling everything changed immediately.

On the Murray the paddle-steamers helped those who were already settled, but the Darling helped with the occupation of the land. With regular transport, pastoralists were happy to set up their sheep grazing, safe in the knowledge their wool could be taken to the cities for sale. The day paddle-steamers arrived in these remote places was a day to celebrate. It was then the settlers would find out what was happening in the big world. They would replenish their stores and browse through a wide range of goods the steamers carried, from women's perfume to the most mundane household requisites.

The Darling also had more turbulent times. Some of Australia's big shearers' strikes were held in towns and stations along the river. Men were lured to the outback with the promise of work on stations but poor pay and the harsh conditions led to disputation and strikes. Jimmy Dickson, captain of the PS *Rodney*, agreed to transport non-union labour to a station near Menindee. Along the journey he was warned about the reception he faced, but he refused to cancel the trip, instead deciding he should take on extra firewood so he wouldn't need to stop and risk being overthrown.

Pearl Wallace's father, William Collins, owned the PS *Fairy* at the time and was asked by shearers to take them down the river for a picnic. Pearl's father knew they really wanted to confront the other shearers on the *Rodney*. To make matters easy, William took the door off his boiler so he could honestly say the boat couldn't move because he couldn't raise any steam.

The next morning he saw smoke in the sky and burnt timber drifting past. The shearers had strung a line across the river and forced the *Rodney* to stop, whereupon they had doused it with petrol and set it on fire. To the cheers of the unionists, and for her place in history, the *Rodney* sank.

I motored up the Darling for a distance then turned and came back, entering the Murray. I did it a few times actually. It felt different being on another river. It was as though the churn of the water as the steamers went through the junction was real; as though I could hear the cries of the crew and passengers as their voices floated across the water.

Late in the evening a distinct feeling of discomfort came over me when I camped near the junction of the Rufus River, Frenchman's Creek and Lake Victoria. At times along the journey the river's ghosts had visited me but this was different, here there were too many; here their presence was tangible. The night was warm and, although a fire was unnecessary, I lit one anyway.

An important link in the whole river chain, Lake Victoria was filled through Frenchman's Creek with water held back by Lock 9 and returned to the Murray through the Rufus River downstream of Lock 7. Water takes twenty-five days to flow from the Hume Dam to the South Australian border and only fourteen days from the Menindee Lakes on the Darling. Without Lake Victoria acting as a dam the flow to South Australia would vary substantially, making it more difficult to supply the state's entitlement.

Lake Victoria was part of the traditional country of the Maraura people and was a central part of their Dreamtime stories. It is estimated that 250 people lived in the area before European occupation, and that they had been there for up to 18 000 years. When the authorities reduced the lake level to repair the regulator in 1994, the remains of thousands of Aborigines were uncovered. Archaeologists said that with 250 people living there at any one time, 15 000 burials could have occurred over 2000 years. Some of the remains found could have been victims of what is known as the Rufus River massacre.

Leaving the fire burning and knowing there was no one to steal my tent or my ute and boat, I headed off towards the lake. We were in daylight saving time, and even though the sun had almost gone the evening was stretching out. The cool night air and the silence was broken only by the occasional crunch of my foot on a stick.

There had been many stories about the slaughter of Aborigines here during the time of big stock movements. The blacks would steal sheep and spear men in retaliation for being shot at by whites.

In 1841 two overlanders, James Inman and Henry Field, ran into three hundred or so marauding Aborigines who forced them to abandon their flock of about four thousand sheep as well as their horses and drays. News of the battles soon reached Adelaide and troops were sent to sort out the problem. Even Charles Sturt, who had had experience in these matters, offered to help. He was definite about how to handle the situation. 'A gun is a poor weapon of defence when once discharged, and, of this, the natives appear to be aware. The bayonet, therefore, is absolutely necessary to meet their rush, but even with a bayonet a single individual can affect but little. It is only by mutual support that attacks are to be successfully repelled.'

South Australian Governor Grey appeared to be sympathetic. He understood there was trouble but he emphasised that all Aborigines held the same rights of British subjecthood as the settlers, and that, 'to regard them as aliens, with whom a war can exist, and against whom Her Majesty's troops may exercise belligerent rights, is to deny that protection to which they derive the highest possible claim from the sovereignty which has been assumed over the whole of their ancient possessions.'

After skirmishes over a couple of months, the final battle took place when overlanders and police took up positions on either side of the river. After intense fighting some of the Aborigines made for the scrub while others hid in the reed beds of the river. Those in the reeds were shot mercilessly. Official reports say that only thirty were killed, but there were many stories of the actual number being well into the hundreds. It was said that their bones were used when buttress walls were formed in the river and souvenirs were plentiful. There was also a time when a skull with a bullet hole could be had for as little as the equivalent of 75 cents.

Back at the camp the sky was fast filling with stars as though someone or something was switching on lights in the dark. Whether my knowledge of the battle was accurate, and whether the numbers of dead were true, didn't seem to matter. I felt the touch of the slight chill wind and imagined somewhere in the distance the sound of water lapping the edge of the lake.

I'd been with the river for a week and we had enjoyed many conversations, even if they were one-sided. My attention appeared to go unnoticed, but I felt sure the river knew of my presence and we had drifted along, both of us content. We agreed that having crossed the border of New South Wales and Victoria with regularity, it was important to mark the crossing into South Australia on the river, not on a road some distance away.

I had become quite attached to my boat by now. It had been surprisingly faithful and reliable on its irregular journeys. The old motor started easily after going in for repairs and tuning before each venture, and the small crack that was the result of scraping an unseen snag near Swan Hill had been welded together again. Boats usually have a name and perhaps mine should have been christened, but I decided against it. Any name would seem banal and trite. The tinnie should remain nameless, undercover, anonymous. It didn't need a name; it needed to be looked after, to be spoken to nicely and it would work with the river to show me what I needed to see. Besides, tinnies don't have names, speedboats and houseboats do, and if there was one thing the tinnie definitely wasn't, it was a speedboat. Anyway there wasn't much room to paint words on the side and 'tinnie' wasn't such a bad name—even if it was shared by every other aluminium boat in the country.

The tinnie, the river and I decided that Devil's Elbow would be the ideal place to start the trip towards the border. It would only take us two days of leisurely travel to reach Lock 6.

The cliffs at Devil's Elbow were not the same as normal cliffs. They were more like large solid dunes. More individual than one large cliff, they had gullies between them and other cliffs behind. The river at Devil's Elbow—and at other, narrower parts along this stretch—was once hazardous for big boats to navigate safely. Most of them reduced speed when approaching, 'dropping' round the bend instead of steaming, otherwise they could quite possibly have run into the bank. With the advent of locks and weirs that problem had long been resolved, even though there were no more steamers. It wouldn't have worried the tinnie anyway.

In the bottom of the tinnie were a fishing rod and a few spinners which would no doubt be just the things to catch that elusive cod, or any other variety of fish for that matter. A slow, methodical trip began, during which all the fishing advice I'd read or received over the years came to mind.

Weather was the first thing. Some said it needed to be hot, or at least warm, for fish to swim about. Then there was the height of the river. Some fishermen say that you catch them on a rising river while others say it needs to be falling. There is a school of thought that insists you need to fish at dusk; others say early morning is the best time. Fishing experts tell you that you need graphite rods and specially sharpened hooks on fluorescent lines that are made of a stringy substance rather than the old catgut. Then there is bait. Some swear by shrimps, while others say yabbies, worms, moths or witchetty grubs are best. Cod have also been caught using frogs, lizards and other creeping things. The latest rage was cheese—not just ordinary cheese, but gorgonzola and, judging by the selection of lures available for sale in any large fishing store, it was no wonder I couldn't catch a cod. The choice was overwhelming. I was glad that the cod couldn't see them all, otherwise they might have become paranoid about which they are meant to like best.

While all the fishing advice was undoubtedly true, some of the best fish were still caught on old rods, with ordinary lines, using hooks that still had dried worms attached from the last fishing expedition. Then again, perhaps this attitude explained my lack of success.

I trailed the lure out and it wobbled along near the bottom. Of course the lure was destined to be lost and soon was. What must have been a large snag gave me the sudden thrill of hooking a big fish then, within an instant, dashed my hopes. Stuff it, I thought, and chucked the rod on the bottom of the boat. Fishing was forgotten for a time as the river, once again, held me in its thrall. It wasn't until I stopped close to where Scottie's Wood Pile used to be that I picked up the rod again.

Scottie's was one of the many places on the river where timber cutters left piles of wood for steamers to pick up. It was also close to the place where the *Gem*, after pulling out from replenishing stocks, was sunk in 1948. After loading up, the *Gem* had struck a snag, sustaining a large hole on the port side. One man died from shock when she went down, but the other passengers were taken safely ashore. Three weeks later the boat was refloated and taken to Mildura, from where it was bought by Swan Hill's Pioneer Settlement over a decade later. In deference to my home town, now also home to the *Gem*, this was surely the right place to camp.

Late in the evening, as the moon shone brightly enough to bait a hook and fire my imagination, I tried my luck again with fishing, to no avail. The shrimp net was successfully used to trap a few small crustaceans, and the cheese looked tasty, but although I had all the requisite items with me—salt, vinegar, lemons, a few tomatoes and a length of silver foil for wrapping—I was obviously not meant to clean a fish and cook it over my fire or bury it in the coals. Perhaps I should have left the ingredients and cooking materials behind. That would have almost guaranteed me a fish.

There are two borders on this stretch of the river. The border of New South Wales goes north from the river and then, later, the South Australian border goes south. Neither is quite where you would imagine it to be. The line designating the border doesn't go straight through the country; there is a difference of some 12 kilometres between them. For that distance, a section of Victoria is south of a part of South Australia which, when I thought about it, was almost incomprehensible. Surveyors who took the wrong position, and bureaucratic arguments between states about who owned what, caused the problem. The dispute was another that went all the way to the Privy Council. And, although it was always assumed, it wasn't until 1993 that the two states agreed that for those 12 kilometres the border went down the middle of the river.

To find the exact New South Wales border was a difficult task, but the Victorian–South Australian border was easy. A white signpost similar to those you see on highways pointed one way to South Australia and the other to Victoria. According to the attached plaque, the Lions Club of Renmark placed it there in 1981.

Just down from the Victorian border was the old Customs House, where all the riverboat captains had to present their clearance papers and pay any duties before moving interstate. It was said that as this was the remotest of all Customs Houses, there were times when 'suitable arrangements' agreeable to both parties were made between the boat captains and the officers. The Customs House operated here for eight months after Federation when all the others had been closed.

The old stone building was now a general store with a large fleet of houseboats moored at the riverfront. At one houseboat three blokes were taking stores on board. The one on the bank handed a number of barbecue packs and a much larger number of slabs to the two on the boat. Locals taking a few days off, and not wanting to go to the Gold Coast or 'anywhere there's people', they told me they'd be gone for a few days so they had to make sure they wouldn't run out.

They also told me about Bunyip Reach, the next stretch of the river. One of the very few sternwheelers on the river, the PS *Bunyip*, with William Randell in command and two barges lashed alongside, caught fire here. Randell jumped overboard when the flames engulfed the wheelhouse and, with the wheel locked, the boat began turning in circles, causing confusion amongst the twenty people on board. Two crewmen drowned and a woman and her child also died. They were buried near where Lock 6 was later built.

This was also where the Chowilla Dam was to be constructed. Millions of dollars were spent on the planning and site works in the 1960s, but nothing eventuated. The dam was to be the biggest and most ambitious project on the river, stretching for five kilometres across the region. A lake 30 kilometres wide and 90 kilometres long would have been created. In 1970 the South Australian Liberal government wanted the proposed Dartmouth Dam to proceed in Victoria, but the Don Dunstan-led Labour Opposition wanted Chowilla. There was such a strong feeling in South Australia about keeping the water for themselves that it helped Dunstan win the election. After a year or so they realised that without a lock no boats could move along the river and a quarter of the water would be lost in evaporation anyway, so no dam was built.

The Aborigines called this place Tjowilla, 'a place of spirits and ghosts'. There was some truth in that. That night I realised I'd had enough of the remote part of the river for a while. Fortunately, I had plans to catch up with some old friends.

I picked up the houseboat at Paringa, the place where Breaker Morant had worked on the original station before he and two other workmen joined the Bushveld Carbineers and headed off to the Boer War. Paringa was a short distance upstream from Renmark, the last town in the Riverland but the first town when entering South Australia from the eastern states.

A small contraption, the houseboat wasn't grand but it was certainly comfortable. Simply a box of aluminium walls, it had a couple more walls on the inside to make a separate bedroom. Glossy veneer panels covered the kitchen sink and cupboards, framed posters of the river hung on one wall and lace curtains were drawn across the window. Small decks on the front and the back were reached through sliding glass doors. After a quick lesson on the correct buttons, dials and switches I set sail—or, rather, motored away from the mooring.

Houseboats are a relaxing way to travel. They don't have screaming engines and they don't mess with the river's calmness. They have plenty of room and, as driving them doesn't take a great deal of concentration, it's a lot easier to take in the surrounds. Daydream, if you like.

The river was now as wide as at any other part of the river, an average width of around 200 metres. With very little current because of the influence of the locks, it was, as my friend Ted Ward would have said, a duck pond, albeit a very large duck pond. Willow trees lined the banks and high cliffs marked where the river had cut around the bends. Dave Turnbull's house was at the top of one cliff.

Dave and I had joined the navy together and hadn't seen each other since that time. The years fell away quickly as I tied up under a willow tree at Dave's river frontage. The climb to the house, where Dave greeted me enthusiastically, was not as arduous as I had imagined it would be. Inside was his wife Celine, together with another of my friends from Vietnam days, Alan Stevens, and his wife Cheryl.

Stevo, as we called him, owned the larger houseboat tied up a few willow trees downstream from mine. He had, like Dave and I, lived a fairly unsettled life after leaving the navy. He'd suffered severe health problems that caused him to reflect on life and give away a mainstream existence to live on the river.

Stevo's dad had been a soldier settler at Robinvale in the eleventh allocation of blocks. Like all the blockies he worked hard, but there were times when the constant stream of labour could be put aside. Sitting his son on the crossbar of his bike he would cycle down to the river where they would always manage to catch a fish. The river was the first thing Stevo could recall seeing and he remembered those days fondly. In his own way he had tried to keep his river adventure alive. A year or so before he had planned to follow Charles Sturt's voyage along the river, or at least as far as possible. With a book about the explorer's journals on board, he had started at the Murrumbidgee junction where Sturt had discovered the river, each day reading the journal, trying to see what Sturt had seen.

'I looked at every tree to try and get a feel for it,' Stevo said, grinning. 'Even if I couldn't, my imagination worked wonders.'

The trip was spread over six months and showed him 'the magnificence of the river' and the way it changed constantly. 'You can be in the same place day after day and, each morning when you wake up, you see something different,' Stevo said. 'Each day the river has a new look, each evening the shadows fall in a different way.' He thought Sturt would be appalled if he saw the river in its present condition. 'When he came across the Murray he called it a broad and noble river. Not sure what he'd say now.'

In one of his many jobs Stevo had worked in Mildura on the paddle-steamer *Wanera*—named as 'wane era' after the paddleboats were waning—when Paddy Hogg was captain. By then the *Wanera* was a tourist boat and a far cry from what Paddy would have been used to in his time. Yet a paddle-steamer, said Stevo, is a paddle-steamer. They would take tourists for weekend trips to Wentworth and up the Darling for a week.

Paddy taught Stevo how to read the river; what the ripples meant, dark and light, where the snags were and how to try to see around the bends. Like other riverboat captains, Paddy could tell by the way ducks flew that a steamer was approaching. 'He always said he was born under a bullrush when anyone asked him, and he knew the river better than most.'

After more than a few beers, the three of us stood silently in the clifftop garden, each of us back off the coast of Vietnam as sixteen-year-old sailors, not knowing what was to become of us but, as sixteen-year-olds do, eagerly thinking about the future. Much had changed for us in the ensuing years. Bodies and minds had become damaged but some things stayed the same. Friendships forged in difficult times remained.

We stared across the wetlands some fifty or more metres below, while further away the river flowed gracefully through the trees. Nothing disturbed the view to the horizon where the sunset spilled across the sky and where the land met the heavens in colours that none of us could describe.

Dave had lived here all his life, and he'd done many things. He'd worked on the Moomba gas fields, run the local iceworks his father had started many years before, and been a professional fisherman.

The typical fishing reach was around three kilometres long and was said to be enough to provide a living for one family. He laughed. 'Almost true.' He and many others had had their fishing licences revoked, even though they were the only primary industry in the country for 150 years that was still viable and had no government subsidy.

When farmers were forced to pull vines out for one reason or another, the government helped out. Then there was drought relief, where subsidies never seemed to end. But, Dave said, the fishermen regulated themselves for 150 years. When things were quiet they worked part time and fished a bit less. I asked if revoking licences had done anything for fishing. 'Not really,' he replied. 'There's just as many fish coming out of the river, only they're doing it illegally now.'

Fishermen in those days were not only fishermen. 'We used to collect information for the fisheries departments on river conditions and fish on a daily basis. Now that's all gone.'

Could he understand when people said that commercial fishing takes too much from the river?

'Yes, I can, but it didn't happen. We had to look after ourselves otherwise it would have all ended, it was sustainable because we had to make it that way.'

Dave thought the river condition wasn't too bad but could easily slip backwards if it wasn't monitored closely. He said they used to rely on the Darling for flushes even though it was dirty water. They got none of that now. 'It's pretty good water here although the further south you go the worse it gets; overusage in every area, all over the country. We're the bottom of the drain.'

Dave waved his hand to indicate the river in the almost faded light. 'You look at that, beautiful and wide, trees that look good, and you say what's the problem. But it's all artificial.' He said the river desperately needed extra flows. 'We are getting saltier here, the river doesn't move between the locks, it's even stagnant at times. It badly needs flushing. It'll stay the same height and look like this but it needs better water.'

The river was a spiritual place for Dave. When you lived and worked on it there was an affinity only those people understood. 'When I was fishing, I never got sick of it. Each piece of the river was different every day. Aboriginal people talk about their land, well to me the river has that too, an enduring nature, sucking you back to it all the time. Once it has you, you can never leave it.'

By now the sun had gone completely and the air was full of the sounds of frogs in the wetlands. Up and down the scales, thousands of nocturnal voices in a croaking chorus of happiness. In the darkness Dave told me that he loved everything the river gave him, even the frogs and their noise.

Above us was an endless black drape with a billion pricks of light while below us an occasional flash of the moon on the wetlands and the river punctuated the blackness. 'How can you tell people what this is like?' Dave asked quietly.

Many bottles of wine later, and after many stories, I staggered down the hill in the moonlight, weaving a zigzag course through the frogs to the houseboat.

Stevo had told me that living on a houseboat had distinct advantages. If you didn't like your neighbours, you could just let go and move. I moved. Not because I didn't like my neighbours, but I wanted to make Loxton in four days. That's where my ute and tinnie would be waiting. As long as there weren't too many stops, or for too long, time wasn't going to be a problem.

Numerous other houseboats of all sizes made their way along the river. One was literally a house on a boat—pitched roof, verandahs and all, the whole thing stuck on pontoons with a couple of outboards at the stern. A couple more were glassed-in monstrosities with just a small place at the front for steering. All those on board the various vessels were clearly enjoying themselves. They came to the Riverland, hired a houseboat for a weekend or longer, then went back to their normal lives. Although they could never really understand the complete river story they loved the experience, which gave them memories they could keep. But houseboats were also a problem. With over eight hundred registered houseboats in South Australia, and many more private ones, the problems were obvious. Although they were supposed to pump out sewage at stations along the river, none of them are required by legislation to keep their grey water—that all goes into the river. Just one more thing the river had to put up with. And South Australians, I considered, should remember that when complaining about the state of the river.

Approaching Renmark it appeared that every second willow tree had a boat under it; every gum tree as well. Johnny Gurr's was tied up under a willow with two stately gums further back on the bank. After tying up at the next willow I walked across the road.

Johnny's real name was Yvonne, but as she had once been a Johnston, everyone called her Johnny. She was a lady elderly in years but with a light in her eyes and a welcoming smile that belied her age. Her small house was stacked with paraphernalia about boats and the river. A framed poster detailing the sinking of the *Titanic* stood against one wall while several pictures of ships and riverboats decorated the others. Johnny laughed. She didn't apologise for the mess because it wasn't a mess, as she knew where everything was.

Johnny and I talked in her small kitchen. She had written extensively about the river, which had been her life for as long as she could remember—since she was four years old to be exact, when, during the Depression, her family saved enough to have a holiday with aunts and uncles camped on the river near the Blanchetown Weir. 'It was a marvellous time, although crossing the weir made me deadly frightened. All that water underneath it with no guardrails, just wooden planks.'

After spending some time overseas Johnny came back to a fruit block near Loxton but soon turned her love of writing into a career as a journalist with the ABC. She had been in Renmark for thirty-five years, and had lived on the river permanently since 1959.

Johnny reckoned that most of the river's problems were caused by overuse of water and, historically, by lack of agreement between states. 'It started in 1855 when Victoria and New South Wales fought over the water; because the New South Wales boundary was on the southern bank, they objected to

Victorians using water even though much of the water came from Victoria's highlands. So then Victoria put weirs on all their tributaries and during one flood a Victorian government official wrote to his New South Wales counterpart and asked him to remove his water from their property.'

Johnny was philosophical. Before irrigation, she said, there was all this water going past everyone and no one was using it. That was clearly a waste, but then using it unwisely was an even bigger waste. 'We take more than we need. We have a glut of wine grapes now and yet they're still planting more. Even simple old me can see it; we keep planting, even with prices dropping and blatant overproduction.'

Johnny said that when people come and see the river around Renmark they wonder what the problems are. But it was quality that counted. Red gums were dying from lack of water and salinity. The levee banks and weirs kept the water in the river channel and it didn't get out to the trees.

'We need another major flood,' she said, 'and if everything coincides it will happen. Then it will wash everything through. It will happen some day, don't worry.'

We talked about those who come to the river for weekends with speedboats and wave boards. While houseboats and slow boats were tolerated because they had a small wake, she thought the river had enough problems at the bends without being damaged further by wave-makers and speedboats.

Johnny hoped people realised that although the river had been around for millions of years mankind was slowly ruining it, just like they have ruined nearly every other river in the world they've settled on. 'People in positions of power don't want to know anything about it but there is going to come a time when governments will have to stop asking and start legislating a bit more. They put signs up around here about speeding. That does a lot of good, doesn't it?' There was no doubt in Johnny's mind that the river would always be around, but she was worried about what condition it might be in.

'Peace like a river,' she replied when I asked what the river meant to her. 'It says that somewhere in the Bible. John, I think; I suppose I should read it to find out.' To her the river was almost like a church. 'I have the troubles of the world on my shoulders yet I get on my boat and I'm at peace in five minutes. I'm at peace with it, I care for it, so should everybody else.'

Johnny was quiet for a minute, then she nodded. 'Forever,' she said quietly. 'Peace like a river, forever.'

Prior to the white man's arrival the Naralte people had lived around Renmark—in fact, the name 'Renmark' is believed to have derived from the Aboriginal words meaning 'red mud'. One early settler noted the locals were friendly and quickly picked up a small amount of English. They also attempted to show the newcomers their methods of hunting.

Much later, Renmark was the place the Chaffey brothers came to when their plans came unstuck in Mildura, forging the first irrigation settlement on the river in 1887.

Renmark was also one of the many places that was home to David Jones, or Possum, as he was better known. This legendary figure of the bush came to Australia from New Zealand in 1924 as a twenty-three-year-old shearer. During the Great Depression, after having his money stolen from the boarding house where he lived, he became a recluse. With no money he couldn't pay for his Worker's Union ticket and so could not work. Disillusioned he turned his back on society and went to live along the river.

For fifty years he roamed between Renmark and Went-worth, living on the banks of the Murray and the Darling in places like hollow logs and under trees, preferring the company of animals to humans. He lived on much the same food that the Aborigines did, with a bit of feral cat and a few rabbits and foxes thrown in for good measure. His habit of climbing trees to avoid people and in search of honey eventually led to his nickname.

Possum was a shy and kind man who did no harm. He didn't accept charity but rather farmers would find fences mended or wood chopped in exchange for a newspaper and matches. He would also look after flyblown sheep or dig burrs out where stock was feeding. He would let farm dogs off their chains. On occasions he would not be seen for months, and when he returned those who were lucky enough to hear him speak were told he had walked to the Murray's mouth, or up to Bourke along the Darling.

Bill Hogg told me he'd encountered Possum a few times. One night he was at a camp with some other river men and saw a shadow in the trees. He watched it for some time before calling out. Possum didn't show himself but Bill knew he'd been there. 'You could just feel it,' he said.

Roma Jones had met Possum as well, only she didn't know it at the time. In Euston she had told me the story of once being alone near the river at Lyrup, just sitting there to find some peace and quiet, when a man emerged from behind a tree. Their conversation was not very long but he was very kind and softly spoken, and he told her a bit about his life. She found out later who he was and said she would have spoken in more depth if she'd known. Then again, she said, 'he'd have left if I tried to do that'.

This extraordinary man died in 1982, and was found slumped against a gum tree on the bank of the Murray River. Aged eighty-one, he had been dead for a number of weeks. The headstone on his grave in a station cemetery simply reads, 'at rest where he roamed'.

I pulled in at the wharf opposite the Renmark Hotel, a community-owned facility built by the Chaffeys to house their workers. Being temperate men, the hotel sold no alcohol, nor did anywhere else in the town, which the Chaffeys had basically owned.

My mooring was a little downstream of the biggest craft I had seen on the river. The *Spirit of the Murray* was on its maiden voyage from Goolwa. With rows of neatly arranged seats like a bus or a plane it was a luxury touring coach on water. The man standing on the wharf taking photographs shook his head and told me incredulously that it could travel at up to 35 kph. A fully booked touring party of retirees was on the trip and the crew unloaded their suitcases to be relayed to the local hotel.

Tim Edmonds, the photographer and a river historian, had lived in Renmark all his life. A soldier settler he was tall and angular with a face flushed from the years in the sun. Tim had a measured way about him and his love for the river was plain to see. As we talked, his mate Jim Brooks, a former taxi driver and café owner who was shorter, rounder and sporting a floppy towelling hat, arrived to see the new craft.

After a few minutes' discussion about why anything on the river needed to go at that speed, the three of us sat on a bench on the riverfront while they told me about their project restoring one of the river's biggest barges, the *Argo*. Tim and Jim laughed and said they were just a couple of old blokes looking for something to do, but I suspected it was more than that.

Tim had done a bit of renovation work on the PS *Industry*, the town's paddle-steamer, so when the sunken *Argo* was retrieved and brought to Renmark he volunteered to be part of the work team. Each Tuesday morning he and a group of similar-aged men would gather at the barge, which was resting on concrete blocks in a homemade dry dock. Much of the work was tedious; for example, all the boards for the hull had to be replaced individually. The men would lie underneath and knock one of the old planks out, go away, measure and cut a replacement and return to fit it. Neither Tim nor any of the others were shipwrights; all they had was the bit of experience gained from various jobs over the years. 'It was an achievement, no doubt,' said Tim. 'Enormously gratifying.'

The three of us jumped in Tim's car and a few minutes later we walked across the plank and onto the wooden deck of the barge. The *Argo* was once used as a pumping station but the vast, cavernous interior was now bare. While paddle-steamers were grander, more flamboyant, barges like this were blue-collar, hardier—the ditch diggers of their day.

Close by, the banks were lined with willows. Tim explained that many had been planted as markers for riverboats as the low country would flood in the old days and paddle-steamers could end up anywhere. They had also consolidated the banks. When we arrived back at the wharf he pointed out a number of willows that protected the bank on the bend from washing away. Behind, there were fifty-six gums that wouldn't have been there if it weren't for the willows.

'We control the water better now,' Tim said. 'It's the best we've had in years. Have a look around, does it look like no one cares?' He said that despite all the publicity he wasn't sure if the river really was dying. He also pointed out that in Sturt's diary it was recorded that the water was too salty to drink in places, so salinity wasn't just a recent thing. 'You do wonder,' he said. 'There are a few parts of seepage that are salty and trees die anyway; not all gums can live to two hundred years.'

Both Tim and Jim said that it was easy to live there.

'Life is pretty peaceful,' said Jim, 'with the river in your blood.'

Tim nodded his agreement. 'Even though you might go away you never really leave it.'

In the noisier parts of the river there was a noticeable lack of bird life. The usual swallows and magpies and the 'kraaking' river gulls were prevalent, of course, but not much more. When it was quieter, even though I was stuck behind the wheel watching out for larger, more unforgiving craft, there were all sorts of ducks—wood, mallard and mountain ducks—as well as countless ibis. Those big white elegant birds tiptoed through the shallows, feeding on the insects by pushing their long black beaks into the soft soil. They flew off and then landed again, lifting their feet and stepping lightly, almost as though they didn't want to damage anything underfoot. A small flock of them had gathered near Lyrup, where it appeared the feeding must have been good.

A small village, Lyrup was the only place still operating under what was quite a significant communal land system. Housed in an old concrete building near the river, the Village Association's only function now was the ownership and operation of irrigation and drainage facilities for the horticultural blocks owned by its members.

Towards the end of the 1890s the South Australian government knew it needed to do something about the many unemployed men who were demonstrating in the streets of Adelaide. Only limited work was available in the city so they decided to establish settlements along the Murray River. Eleven settlements were proposed with Lyrup being one of the first. Forty men and their wives were selected for the experiment, along with forty-nine single men and 114 children. At the government's expense they were taken by train to Morgan, then to Lyrup on the PS *Ellen*. The settlers were left on the bank with food supplies, bedding, furniture and tarpaulins so they could make tents or shelter of some kind. The settlers must have been glad to be there as they gave the captain and crew a rousing cheer as the paddle-steamer departed. The next week the PS *Gem* delivered iron, timber, ploughs and other heavy items that could not be fitted onto the *Ellen*.

The group elected people to be in charge and soon enough this new collective farming enterprise became established. Groups of around twenty people combined resources and worked for the common good. Each family could draw up to 10 shillings a week for hard groceries but the rest had to be grown. With water from the river, vegetables grew quickly, there was plenty of wood for fires and to build shelter, and the river had plenty of fish, the forest plenty of rabbits and other game.

But it didn't last. They battled flies, mosquitoes, scorching summers and freezing rainy winters. Many of these settlers had been born in England or other European countries and these were unbelievably primitive conditions. The often-violent arguments between families caused the whole system to break down. Some battled through while others took their own lives. The scheme was supposed to last for thirteen years; it lasted two. Those who stayed through the difficult period became much tougher and the land never beat them.

The *Murray River Charts* had stopped at Renmark and my guide now was the *Murray River Pilot*. These charts were drawn by Ronald and Margaret Baker, with William Reschke's words accompanying them. The book was perched in front of the houseboat's wheel, giving an indication of my whereabouts while driving.

The river floodplain in these parts is up to 10 kilometres wide, part of what was once called Bungunnia. A giant freshwater lake of some 33 000 square kilometres which had appeared and disappeared before the advent of humans, Bungunnia was formed about two million years ago when the lower Murray was dammed by an earth uplift. The lake emptied about 700 000 years ago, but both before and after, over 60 million years, the river had worn through the ground, leaving above it the striped cliffs under which I camped. According to the charts, I was in an area known as Willabalangaloo.

This was where Dad and I came fishing when we lived nearby. When we would load up the old van that he'd scraped together the money to buy. When we weren't burdened by expectation and when we'd listen to the cricket on a small plastic transistor radio tuned to the ABC.

I decided to try fishing in the spot where my father had once caught a five-kilogram cod. We didn't have fishing rods then, just old twine handlines. Sinkers were made from the lead in old batteries that we melted down in a discarded pot, poured into an old spoon then dunked in a tin of water. The hole for the line was made by hammering a nail through the top.

Dad would wind his line up like a hammer thrower and heave it out with a shrimp or a yabbie attached that must have become quite dizzy before it hit the water. Then he'd wait. I would too. Perhaps that's why I was no good at fishing. I learnt daydreaming techniques from my father. The cod he caught was the unluckiest fish in the river. He must have been swimming along and just swallowed the bait. The cod caught himself, but the smile on Dad's face when he pulled it in lit up the cliffs like the morning sun.

Now I had a rod, a decent reel, bait from a proper bait shop, and sinkers of differing shapes and sizes with special gold-coloured wire attachments for the line. The hooks were special ones sold by a man who promised faithfully that if there was a fish nibbling at the bait, these were the hooks to catch it. I fished for hours, or rather my line was in for hours. My mind had drifted back forty years or so while the fish swam past unharmed.

I guided the houseboat under the bridge at Berri and tied up near the concrete steps cut into the river bank. The bridge was relatively new, but the concrete steps were old. They were part of what used to be the local swimming pool. A fenced-off area in the river, it once had a diving board at one end with a small ladder to the top which, to an eleven year old, seemed frighteningly high. In the summer the water dripping from youngsters' bodies would mark the concrete steps for about three seconds before it disappeared with the heat.

Sitting on the steps reminded me of a childhood game. We would dive off the board and down into the depths where the fence poles had a gap that we'd wriggle through before coming up for air on the other side. The danger was apparent to adults but not to us. Then there were summer days when we'd swim across the river to the bank where there were no willows, only gum trees. There was once a punt across the river, but the new bridge had taken its place. Sometimes we'd jump off the side of the punt and let the current sweep us down underneath before we surfaced. The really daring amongst us would dive from the front of the punt and wait underwater until it had passed over us. The punt driver didn't seem to care; he encouraged us, laughing at our gasps as we surfaced and waving while the clanking machinery dragged the laden ferry to the opposite bank.

I moved further along the bank, close to the place in the bullrushes where I would sit and hide from the world, listening to the river talk to me through its ripples. Where I would watch the birds and listen to the wind in the trees. Where the colours of the morning and the evening inspired feelings of awe. And where the darkness of the night helped when things were wrong.

Although Berri was a town in the early 1900s, it wasn't until the soldier settlers came after both world wars that it grew, as did nearly all the towns in the Riverland. These places also saw a great increase in what was known as 'river migration' when men and their families would make their way along the river—the Murray Whalers again—and eke out a living until they found somewhere they could obtain some land. A large number were migrants.

Glossop was a few kilometres inland and, after locking up the boat and making sure the mooring ropes were tied securely, I walked through the vaguely familiar streets of Berri and stood, thumb out, hoping for a lift.

A truck pulled up shortly after, the driver and I exchanging pleasantries. He hadn't been in the area long so I didn't tell him much; he probably wouldn't have understood anyway. He dropped me off at the Glossop store and I walked to the street where we had lived. It wasn't as far away as I'd remembered, although when you're older a thousand paces don't take you as far as they do when you're young.

The house was still there, surrounded by the vines and trees. The verandah and sleepouts still had the flywire; the garden was still bare. The road was now bitumen, although at the edges of the black tar, the dirt felt the same. A worker in the vineyard stopped and watched me for a minute or so, then went back to his tasks. After returning to the shop and then walking down the lane to the schoolyard, I sat under a familiar peppercorn tree and thought about Jimmy.

I'd never been really close to a black person before, and Jimmy was very black. We sat under a big gum tree and I watched his face as he drew circles with his finger in the hot red soil. His eyes were like glazed marbles set deep in his shiny face. The new plastic sandals I was wearing were rubbing and the soil was getting in the sides, burning my feet. It must have been 105 in the waterbag. Jimmy had taught me that expression. He thought I should learn some Australian sayings. He started scraping together handfuls of soil and watched them as they poured onto the ground through a funnel of clenched fingers, all the while looking at the ground, never at me.

Jimmy was thirteen, a couple of years older than me but wiser by centuries. I had met him on my first day at school. He took me to assembly and stood quietly as a couple of boys played drums while the Australian flag was raised. Then they all sang about southern skies gleaming with a thousand eyes—all of them except Jimmy and me. On the way back to the classroom he told me that the only thing worse than being a pom in that school was being a blackfella. He seemed to be alone so I sort of gravitated to him. I felt the same.

At lunch time, Jimmy would head for the gum trees down the back of the school where he hoped no one would bother him and, because he was my only friend, I would go too. There we'd sit, talking sometimes but mostly silent, him playing with his soil and me watching. Until they came.

They weren't bigger than us but they were confident. I'd never known bullying or been much of a fighter but Jimmy was used to it. He'd do pretty well most days, although he couldn't fight them all at once and I was pretty useless. They thought he was fair game and that I had to be tested out. After all, I was a foreigner. Maybe they thought we both were. Once, afterwards, Jimmy said we should take it in turns. He'd go to the other end of the yard one day and hide and I could go the next. They must have got a bit bored with trying to find us and after a few days they left us alone. Now we could sit in peace under the big sugar gums where the smell of the leaves and the soil lingered in your nose for hours.

We were watching a sleepy lizard meander through the gums one day when Jimmy told me to come home with him after school and meet his grandfather. Clarence was a big man. Huge, black and clever. I could see where Jimmy learnt everything. Clarence taught me a lot about the strange new land I was in. He showed me the different birds and animals, where to look for a fish and how to get a feed out of the river. We would sit for hours on the bank of the Murray and talk, just Jimmy, Clarence and me. And when we tired we would lay down and listen to the sound of magpies singing like unoiled cartwheels.

After a few weeks the kids at school saw that perhaps I wasn't as bad as they had thought and I was accepted more and more. One day, after being away for a week, I ran down to the gum trees to see Jimmy. He seemed distracted. He was obviously unhappy, so I asked him why. Not looking up he said, 'You're one of them now. You're an Aussie and I'm still a blackfella.'

I changed schools soon after that and I never saw Jimmy or any of the others again. I hoped Clarence taught other kids the way he taught Jimmy and me. I hoped Jimmy stayed the same when he grew up. I hoped he didn't become too cynical. Most of all I hoped the other kids had changed.

A large gathering of well-dressed people was outside a marquee on the riverbank by the time I returned. After moving the houseboat even further downstream away from the crowd, I changed into my suit and tie and returned for the function.

The Chefs of the Murray concept was introduced by the Murray River Tourism group, whose members came from the food and wine industry right along the river. Designed to teach young chefs how to prepare the produce available thanks to the river, the group gave these youngsters opportunities to cook for large gatherings and to be mentored by chefs of the calibre of Stefano de Pieri. The Riverland had joined the initiative and I had been invited to their inaugural dinner.

I had been to a previous Chefs on the Murray function at home on a late January evening when we boarded the paddle-steamer *Pyap* for a short trip up the river while listening to an Italian accordionist, eating hors d'oeuvres and tasting wine. When the day was winding down after reaching well over 40 degrees, we dined on the banks of the river in a marquee with the sides lifted. The evening was stuffy and hot, a typical mallee day where the heat makes you feel as though you've walked around all day with your head in an oven. This was different, but the river was still the guest of honour.

The evening was cooling down as Leon Fielke—one of many who lived in the Riverland with names the origins of which were other than Anglo-Saxon—took his seat beside me. Leon's wife Sam was one of the evening's organisers and was too busy to spend much time sitting down, so Leon and I were left to discuss the first few bottles of wine without her. He sipped and looked and smelt and swirled. He knew what he was doing. I had no idea about any of that, but they all tasted good to me.

Another at our table was Bill Moularadellis, a short, immaculately dressed winery owner whose father had emigrated from Greece in the 1950s with nothing. After Stefano made a welcoming speech, he and Bill shared a bottle with me, as well as their thoughts. Stefano said the river was regarded as an icon but, even so, did not get the recognition it deserved. In his speech he had said that nights like these were important for helping young people with their careers, but also to promote what the river gives to the country. 'It starts in the cold weather of the mountains and finishes in the heat of South Australia. It has such a diversity of products, from milk to brandy to grapes to lemons to limes to stone fruit and to berries. We must let the world know about it.'

Both men agreed that those who use the river for utilitarian purposes couldn't really care about it. As Bill said they use it, soil it, drop litter in it and then go back to the city or wherever. Bill said that he spent time at the river 'just to be'. He regularly sat on the bank, ate his lunch, then went back to the office and, no matter how stressed he had been before lunch, everything was all right again. 'It's a very personal thing, the spirituality comes when you connect with it personally and everybody has a different connection. It's like the blood in my veins, the water gives me my life.'

One of the reasons Bill respected the river was that when he travelled any distance from it, when he saw the barren clay landscape out in the backblocks, he knew that without the river the landscape around his property would be no different.

Bill was concerned with the river's health but in a different way to Stefano. 'As wine producers we have regulations which are quite appropriate. But where are the regulations for cattle farmers and all the stuff their herds throw up that finds its way into the river?' Bill warmed to his subject. 'And the cultivation of land that is washed through into the river. I walked down to the river on my block the other day and on the other bank was a herd of sheep drinking and walking in the river and crapping and pissing in it. If there was a toilet or a drinking fountain there would be an absolute outcry, but in the catchments that's almost what it is. What vision and what commitment do we have if we can't control or legislate for that?'

Both men said there needed to be an inclusive attack without everyone waiting for someone else to do the work.

'It mustn't be us and them,' said Stefano. 'It's a collective, it's us.'

Rose Kemp, another of the organisers, sat next to me as the entrée was served. Rose had been involved in helping the Chefs of the Murray develop a constitution. As with many organisations, many people with differing skills were involved in the whole process. Rose gave the skills she had used in helping others develop their constitution.

'We all have a love for the Riverland,' she said, 'and this is the right idea for the right time.'

The consensus in the marquee was that a few years earlier, when the area was struggling economically, it would have been harder to achieve a focus such as this. With more affluent times emerging, everyone wanted to protect what they had. And it was clear to them all that underlying everything was the river. Rose was especially practical. 'If the river stopped flowing or got into huge trouble health-wise, this would all go and go quickly. It goes without saying that we must look after it.'

As well as being practical and prosaic, Rose had a keen sense of the river's effect on her spirtually. She said there was an intrinsic way you get wiser as you get older, and you think about things in a more metaphysical way. That you understand your sense of place a bit more and what it all means. 'The river gives me a sense of understanding what the Aboriginal people mean when they talk to me about their connection with the land and their Dreaming.'

Rose said the river was alive. 'I watch it every morning, to see if it's dead smooth or moving or whether it has risen or fallen or whether the winds are whipping it up. It's part of me.'

Rose excused herself and went to talk to someone important while I looked out of the marquee at the river. Tim

Edmonds, the photographer I'd spoken to in Renmark, was right in a way. When you saw the banks and the trees and the boats it was hard to believe anything was wrong. But dig a bit deeper and you find threats like dying trees and salt and man-made pollution.

Rose returned and I asked if she thought the river knew all the things we spoke about. To me the river was happy tonight but did its state of mind coincide with summer and winter? With calmness and stormy weather? Was it happy on a pleasant day and was it angry and upset when it was rough? Was it especially happy when it had water or when it was in flood?

Rose smiled calmly. 'That's a bit deep for me. Perhaps all this is the way the river lets us know it's happy. It's saying, "here see what I can do if you look after me".'

I suspected she wasn't being quite honest. How could she have that special connection with the river and not feel something similar. Rose smiled and walked away.

Omer Najar sat down in the seat Rose had vacated. A swarthy, bearded man whose face held a constant smile, Omer's family had migrated from Lebanon in 1934, following his uncles who had arrived in the 1890s. He laughed infectiously and said that in the 1890s there were good reasons to leave Lebanon and, 'let me tell you, a hundred years hasn't changed much'. His predecessors were hawkers, wandering through the towns along the river and further into the outback selling anything they could get their hands on.

Omer admitted that he hadn't thought much about water until the drought had meant their water allocations were cut back. 'It was a part of life; I was born here and the river went past us. But when you realise it's not just there but a necessity, it becomes something you think about a lot more.'

Omer had a boutique winery in Monash and didn't admit to any mystical thoughts about the river until I asked him what it meant. He rubbed his beard and grinned again. 'You're right, it is more than I thought. Early on it was just for recreation but then it changed to a feeling of not wanting to use it just as a utility. It's more than just water.'

Later, as the wine flowed more freely and the conversation turned to matters more practical than philosophical, I left the tent and went to spend some time with Jimmy James.

An Aboriginal tracker, Jimmy James was a Pitjantjatjara man who came to the Riverland to live at the Gerard Mission. For over thirty years he worked with the police, tracking and helping capture many criminals as well as finding other souls who had been lost in the bush. It was said that to him, reading the bush was like reading a paper. Jimmy was sensitive, caring and had a generosity of spirit that endeared him to all. He died in 1991 and was buried in Berri.

A monument had been placed on the river a short walk from the marquee. Two slabs of granite marked the spot. One bore images of birds and animals—a crow for his mother, a black hawk for his father, as well as a water tortoise, goanna, stumpy-tailed lizard and the great cod, Ponde. A snake representing the river wound its way around them all. Jimmy's life-sized bronze face was concentrating on the ground, his hand pointing the way.

Would Jimmy James have known my Jimmy? Would he have been friendly with Clarence? Could he have helped them when they lost their way?

Back on the houseboat the air was motionless. The stars danced on the water, the shadows from the gum trees that were, like me, younger when I lived there, fell through the moon's glow. The night was full of mystique, and my thoughts turned to Paul Simon, who once wrote that even after changes upon changes we are more or less the same.

Making your way through a lock is a particularly satisfying experience, especially when it is the first time. Entering Lock 4 on the high side I floated in there for about ten minutes while another craft, much grander than mine, made its way towards the weir. As we waited, the lock master chatted to me. He said the locks were not used much after the riverboat trade dropped away following World War II. From then until the 1960s Lock 4 had moved an average of five boats a year. Then houseboats became popular, and now most locks in the region handled over two thousand craft annually.

The locks from Blanchetown to Mildura created a series of stepped pools, each raising the level of the river by some three metres, each helping to achieve permanent navigation. Opened by hydraulic-powered arms, the lock gates are closed again after boats have entered. When the water level is the same on both sides, the gates at the front are opened and boats sent on their way. The Chinese used locks similar to this in the eighth century, then Leonardo da Vinci designed another bearing an even closer resemblance to these. Operation was simple. The gates formed a V shape against the current and the water pressure from upstream helped to keep them closed, while the pressure of water within the lock kept the downstream gates closed.

The other boat in the lock was almost one big tinted-glass window and, although I waved in its general direction, I could see no obvious signs of life. A couple of shadowy figures flitted around inside but no one ventured onto the decking. I was tempted to go down and see them but thought better of it. After all, it was apparent they wanted nothing to do with anyone else. An uncommon occurrence, because there was usually an instant bond between people on the water.

Once the bigger boat was in place, the gate closed and the lock master dropped the water level, opened the front gates and away I went. The procedure had taken a bit over half an hour and I settled down to the continuation of a long day. Driving a houseboat almost 40 river kilometres with only yourself to steer—and with a hangover—is not ideal. Yet, at only eight kilometres an hour it was reasonably pleasant. I could watch the world float by, listen to the birds, see what the lunatics in their speedboats were doing and take note of the sandbars and cliffs. Even though the river twisted and turned as though it had no idea of where it should be heading, travelling downstream helped me make good time. After stopping a number of times and enjoying the silence and the feel of a few sandbars, I reached Loxton just on dusk. A willow tree at Habel's Bend provided the perfect mooring. Soon, to the sound of nearby kookaburras, the sun fell completely from view, and the reflection of the trees disappeared from the face of the water.

Early summer

Loxton to Morgan

The opening of the cod season is 1 December, when hundreds of fish hunters flock to the rivers—most of them to the Murray and other rivers around Swan Hill. There are more camps on the river and more tinnies on the water than at any other time of the year. Packing a couple of rods, lots of tasty bait—including the most expensive cheese in the supermarket—I headed off up the river determined to come home with a fish. Late that night, after about nine hours of watching and waiting, I went home with nothing. The three European carp that attached themselves to my lines had, by law, to be killed and not returned to the water. Totally disillusioned, the only thing was to give fishing away for a few days and head back to Loxton.

Loxton derived its name from a stockman who used a hut there in the early days. In 1907 Loxton's Hut dropped both the 's and the Hut. When the government opened up the land, most of the pioneers to the area were of German origin. These hardy settlers came and battled the unrelenting dry, the dusty red soil and the ever-present poverty. They were granted small tracts of mallee land that grew small amounts of grain in years when small amounts of rain fell, but which otherwise were drought-stricken and rabbit-infested. Eventually they stopped trying to grow totally unsuitable European varieties of wheat and began to plant newer, Australian-developed strains. These varieties were successful and life, although still a constant battle, became easier. Shortly after World War I the railway arrived and the wheat could be sent reliably rather than depending on the vagaries of the riverboat trade.

During World War I the local council—who also were mostly of German lineage—all pledged allegiance to King and country, although there was some consternation amongst those locals of English heritage. The Lutherans decided, pragmatically, that they should hold their church services in English as well as German.

When World War II broke out, locals treated it very seriously, even though it was on the other side of the world. Loxton even formed its own Home Guard and dug air-raid shelters. But nothing happened and Loxton's war was reasonably quiet and safe. The town flourished when, like other places along the rivers, the government decided it was to be another of the Riverland's soldier settlement irrigation communities.

A short distance away from the main part of town, a group of obviously retired men were repairing a roof on one of the buildings in the Loxton Historical Village. They went steadily about their work; three balanced on top of the building doing what appeared to be all the work, while three below handed up tools, materials and plenty of advice. From my vantage point 50 metres away on a small rise overlooking the village and the river, the staff dressed in pioneer costumes made the village look the way it might have a hundred years before.

Further down the river, through a stretch of parkland in the Loxton Riverfront Caravan Park, was what the locals called the Tree of Knowledge, an ancient gum tree that bore small signs marking the height of all the flood levels down the years. A number of years were grouped closely together while, further up the trunk, were the years 1974, 1975 and 1973. A metre or so above that was 1931, while two metres higher still was the great flood of 1956. Towns from Mildura to Mannum suffered that year when the rampaging river swept through them.

After being on the river for so long, driving the ute again felt strange. The river meant coolness most of the time, with at least a self-created breeze, but in the non-airconditioned ute there was just the unrelenting heat of summer. After having water underneath them for a week my feet felt quite different on top of the bitumen road. They regained their composure quickly, though, and half an hour after leaving Loxton I made a small detour into the Daisy Bates Reserve.

Daisy, who had lived with Aboriginal people in the outback for many years, had at the age of seventy-three pitched a tent here to prepare her papers for presentation to the national archives. The reserve was peaceful, a place for quiet reflection, even though a small flock of cockatoos sitting in a tree were in full cry.

Then two jet skis zoomed up. One powered its way straight down the river while the other criss-crossed its wake, bounding over the small waves. A few hundred metres further on they changed places, then turned around and headed back. The noise of their engines faded eventually, leaving only the waves created by their antics slapping sadly against the bank. Concern for

Daisy Bates's spirit was put aside as I drove away from the river to the small village of Loveday.

During World War II 'enemy aliens' were interned by the Australian government across the country. Loveday was the site of South Australia's main camp. Internees were kept in three compounds and three wood camps. Mostly of German, Italian and Japanese origin, they were joined in the camps by a number of prisoners of war. The first detainees arrived in 1941 and two years later there were over five thousand. The last were set free early in 1946.

The internees grew plants for the production of rubber, pyrethrum for making insecticide and opium poppies for morphine, all of which were vital during wartime. They also grew vegetables and propagated many varieties of seed for both army and civilian use. The wood gathered at the three wood camps went to fire the steam pumps used on the local irrigation blocks.

Internees didn't have to put up with barbed wire and guards all the time. From 1943, for instance, Italian prisoners were billeted out as farm labourers. They worked without guards, under the supervision of the nearest control centre, and received a weekly wage of one pound. Some of these internees were men who had migrated to the area, started their farms and then been locked up. It seemed ironic that they'd been forced to cut wood to supply boilers that would irrigate farms which they would eventually go back to work on.

When Japanese prisoners were caught in the floods at Murtho, a wood camp, the captain of the PS *Kelvin*, Bob Reed, rescued them and their guards. I suspected there would have been many at the time who would have agreed with him helping the guards but may have debated the rest of the rescue.

There wasn't much to see at Loveday—no camps, no fences. Everything was now private property, although at the place that had served as the headquarters a few intriguing buildings and some ruins remained.

After navigating the river through many of its twists and turns I felt compelled to take the tinnie on the longest straight the Murray had had—the seven-mile reach. From Windmill Bend I could see straight down the river. Nothing impeded the view, apart from the distance my eyes could focus. The banks narrowed at times but mostly it was straight navigation. I was happy; the river would have been as well. We were both in cruise control, not having to worry about going around corners or our wake washing banks away, nor about how deep the river needed to be to avoid snags. It was just straight, carefree boating; the sun beating down, the wind in my face and hair, and the tinnie skimming across the water like a stone.

Halfway along the reach was New Residence, another of the experimental towns like Lyrup. All the other places had distinctive names, but New Residence sounded decidedly unimaginative.

After passing the more lyrically named Moorook, I decided to make my next stop at the wonderful-sounding Cobdogla, home to the unique Humphrey Gas Water Pump, a quite extraordinary feat of engineering. Housed in the Cobdogla Irrigation Museum, this was the result of a trip to London in the early years by the South Australian Director of Irrigation. The pumps he saw were so impressive he ordered a couple that ended up here at Cobdogla. Halfway around the world they came, from London to Cobdogla, and someone had forgotten to pack instructions. Normally that would have caused problems but it didn't faze the local engineer at all. He used his ingenuity to work his way around things and soon the pumps were in use.

How the pump worked with gas and pressure valves and other technical stuff was beyond a Luddite like me but it looked extremely impressive. A sign at the pumphouse said the pumps were started occasionally and, even though it was reputed to have been able to launch water 200 tonnes at a time, looking at a giant pump throwing that amount of water around was not of much interest to me. Instead, I sat near the river and said 'Cobdogla' out loud a number of times, listening to the way it sounded and the way it rolled off my tongue.

The trailer bounced alarmingly in a deep pothole on the track through the grey mudflats near Overland Corner, causing the gear in the tinnie to appear in the rear-vision mirror. Daydreaming was not only confined to fishing. I slowed immediately, as it was important that everything stayed in the boat for the journey to Waikerie.

When Australia was still developing there were large movements of cattle driven from the east by overlanders to the new colony of South Australia. Drovers rested their herds at Overland Corner, allowing them to fatten up on the river flats before embarking on the final part of the journey to Adelaide. Prospectors heading the other way to the gold rush in New South Wales also stopped here. Paddle-steamers visited regularly, supplying settlers and goldminers in both states. They returned with wool from the outback stations.

Steamers needed huge amounts of wood to fire their boilers so a certain William Brand started a riverside woodpile, and before long a few cattle duffers, escaped convicts and the odd bushranger had moved into the district. The government then opened a police station among the other few buildings, the most long-lasting of which was the Overland Corner Hotel, built by William Brand and his brother Henry. It was still frontier country, and when William turned up one day with his new bride it is said that almost three hundred Aboriginal women turned up to see the 'whitefella gin'.

After launching the tinnie and restowing the gear in the correct places, I walked back to have a look around the hotel. Its limestone walls and red gum floors and pillars hadn't changed since Brand began his woodcutting venture. The wooden doors bore the pockmarks and dignity of age and artifacts from the period were displayed in tiny rooms with low ceilings. A newspaper cutting here, a pocket watch there; a flask, a lantern and a knife. Old photographs meant the harshness of the times had been captured for all to study a hundred years later.

One of the most retold stories about the hotel concerned the bushranger Captain Moonlight, who spent some time around the Corner during 1879. Said to have ridden into the pub on his horse, he instructed other drinkers to leave both front and rear doors open so he could make a hasty getaway if the troopers appeared. Eventually he moved to New South Wales where he was caught and hanged.

In the garden a black box tree said to be two hundred years old spread ancient arms comfortingly across the modern tables and umbrellas. Its branches, with burls and knots and twists and wrinkles, looked like an aged body. Close by, in the official cemetery, William Brand, his wife and child lay side by side.

As midafternoon came on the first hot day of summer, rain clouds drifted in, and combined with the sun beating down relentlessly, the humidity was at once debilitating and regenerative. The first days of any season have their own feel, taking you to places that flit around your memory, waiting to emerge when the time is right. Hot days on the river are one such time. The trees showed no signs of movement and the glare from the water made me squint. The metal of the boat sizzled when water splashed on it and, when I slowed, flies came from everywhere, buzzing obnoxiously around my face, undeterred by any spray. Ah, the wonders of summer.

Being back on the water was enjoyable. Between Swan Hill and Mildura towns had appeared only intermittently. Since then it had been almost like driving along a country highway and entering a city, leaving the open, less populated spaces for constant built-up areas.

Now the river and me were alone again in one of its most flat, wide and beautiful stretches. A kilometre or two inland was barren country, a constant reminder of how remote this part of the country would be without the river cutting through it. There was nothing around; Lock 3 was 10 river kilometres behind me while Lock 2 was 40 kilometres ahead.

Slowing down simply to reach out and touch the cliffs was quite an experience. It was easy to see why this part of the river was known as the Murray Gorge. Full of shells, corals and, apparently, the odd fish skeleton, these works of limestone art were formed millions of years before when the area was covered by sea, before the river gradually wore its way down. Shell fossils abounded but I saw no fish skeletons. Even when they'd been dead for millions of years, fish had a way of avoiding me.

The river reminded me a bit of how it was back in Swan Hill. While it was a lot wider here and the scenery was different, it had a similar air of solitude. There were no speedboats, in fact there were no boats of any kind, except one; a wide-hulled wooden vessel aground on a sandbar that I came across a couple of hours into the journey.

Steering over and pulling alongside, I called out to the grizzled old river man who waved back with no great enthusiasm. He hobbled over with a roundish gait, his shoulders stooped and swinging, almost protecting himself against the overuse of his hips, which appeared to need attention.

His boat was similar to him: weathered. With paint peeling off the hull and the superstructure badly in need of refurbishment, it didn't appear to be at its most seaworthy—if river boats could be said to be seaworthy, that was.

We didn't exchange names; it seemed superfluous. He told me his boat was an old milk scow that in the 1930s had been used around the lower reaches of the river. Dairy farmers would put milk churns out each night and morning on small jetties and the scow would collect them. A covered-in section had been added later.

'History,' he said, looking at his craft lovingly. 'History.'

He pointed to the flag flying from the pole on the stern. 'The Lower Murray flag,' he informed me. 'Different from the Upper Murray flag because of where the stars are and the colour of the blue bars.'

My new-found friend clambered back on board, re-emerging with a crumpled, water-stained sheet of tourist information. It said the origins of the two flags are not known but the Lower Murray one probably came into use when the Murray River League was formed in 1850. It was certainly in use when William Randell's *Mary Ann* began her voyage upstream. The flag was also flown on the barge *Eureka* when it was sunk in 1853. Interestingly, there was a similarity between the stars on the river flag and those on the flag flown at the Eureka Stockade in 1854.

The four blue stripes are said to represent the four main rivers in the Murray–Darling Basin—the Murray, Murrumbidgee, Darling and Lachlan. The three white stripes represent the states of Victoria, New South Wales and South Australia. The different colour blue supposedly indicated the difference between the waters of the Murray and the Darling.

The information was fascinating, I assured him—but what was he doing out here?

'Just having a spell,' he replied, almost willing me to leave but being too polite to say so. 'Just to be by meself.'

Not long afterwards I was, according to the *Murray River Pilot*, on a sandbar near Good Hope Landing at the start of the Great Yarra Reach. Being nothing if not determined—or bloody-minded—I got out the fishing rod, threaded on a worm and threw the line out.

In summer, sandbars were a part of the lives of everyone who lived on the river. Barbecues (or picnics on fire-ban days), beach chairs set up in the shallows, fishing rods stuck in the sand and checked very occasionally, were all part of the weekend. As was wandering away and exploring in the trees on the banks and trying desperately to see how far you could tip-toe across the burning sand without wearing thongs. And swimming.

After the line had been thrown out for the fish to ignore, I immersed myself in the healing river. Sea water has its own feel but standing on a sandbar, wriggling your toes in what was once a beach of an inland sea and lowering yourself into the coolness of the deep, abiding water of the Murray is something else entirely. There is also something strangely affirming about swimming when there's no one else around. Stroking slowly out to the middle I looked back at the bank, absorbing the totally new perspective both up and downstream from my position close to the water's surface.

Swimming made me think of Tammy van Wisse. I had met her in Swan Hill when she came up to help host the Chefs of the Murray event on that hot summer evening the year before. Tammy knew all about swimming in the Murray. In 2001 she became the first person to swim from Bringenbrong Bridge to Goolwa, including a gruelling crossing of Lake Alexandrina, in an incredible 106 days—almost 23 kilometres a day. Tammy spent a total of 472 hours in the water with an average 72 strokes per minute, with a total of over two million.

Like Stefano de Pieri, Tammy was an official Murray River Ambassador and, even though she had always loved the river, she had gained a special affinity during her swim. 'It was difficult at times, but there was something about the river that helped me, I'm sure.'

Tammy started her swim in the snowmelt from the Snowy Mountains where she could see her hands in the clear, cool water. The further she swam the saltier, murkier and muddier the water became. Hypothermia was a problem at the start of her swim but by the end the temperature was well over 40 degrees. Tammy thought the whole experience was incredible and she developed an enormous respect for the river; 'I know that when it's sick, everyone suffers.'

Tammy agreed with Stefano. She was adamant that the river needed everyone to work together. 'We need a strategy that is above politics and state boundaries.'

Back on the bank the wet patches on the sand were soaked up instantly. I reeled in my line, rebaited the hook that was shiny and devoid of any food whatsoever, and chucked it out again.

Local Aborigines called the river Murrundi. Known as the Indi near its source, it was the Millewa around Echuca and the Milloo near Swan Hill. In the gathering dark, as the river lost the sun's sparkle and gained that of the heavens, I thought about the local Dreamtime legends, Ngurunderi and Ponde.

Ngurunderi was a Dreamtime hero who travelled down the Murrundi in a bark canoe searching for two wives who had left him. At the time the river was only a stream below the

Darling junction. Ponde, a giant fish, swam ahead widening the river with great sweeps of his tail. Ngurunderi chased Ponde trying to spear him but Ponde darted from side to side, creating bends and twisting and turning to keep away from the spears.

Ngurunderi landed a couple of spears and these formed the fins on Ponde's back. The spears made Ponde twist and turn and flap even more at times until finally he swam into Lake Alexandrina where, with the help of Nepele, a spirit brother of Ngurunderi's wives, he was speared and died. Ngurunderi then divided Ponde with his stone knife, each piece creating a new species of fish. When Ngurunderi threw the last piece in the water he declared, 'You can go on being Ponde.'

An Aboriginal friend of mine, Terry Atkinson, told me that story. We would often sit by the river or at his home, and he'd tell me about some of his people's legends. Or we'd walk through the red gum forest and listen to the silence. He would show me the bush tucker trees while flocks of sulphur-crested cocka-toos shattered the peace with their maniacal screeching. He taught me parts of the Wamba Wamba language, spoken by the people who lived around Swan Hill.

'Purt' instead of smoke came from my fire and each morning I saw the 'pirnang nyawi' rise in the east. Regardless of the time of year I knew it was a waste of my time trying to catch a 'pandyil' and sometimes when I was alone, remembered that home was 'malanga'—far away.

Terry was a harmless larrikin as well as a talented sign-writer. His mind was much deeper than he was given credit for and he taught his kids well. He always told his children to treat people with respect, no matter what they said. He advised them not to respond to the insults and one day they would know why. I hoped he was right.

'I will be, mate,' he'd grin. 'I will be.'

The sun was even hotter the next morning and the sand warmed up quickly. The sweat was welcome. Later in summer it wouldn't be, and I'd be longing for the cooler weather, but now it cleaned out the pores and reminded me, as ever, of what the next few months would be like.

Time in the tinnie passed while listening to music through the earphones on my new battery-powered CD player. A couple of enjoyable hours were spent in the company of Bob Dylan, whose words had come to me the evening before when sounds of the night came from all around. When it was just like the night to play tricks while I was trying to be so quiet.

Then I hit the snag. It came out of nowhere. I had been looking behind me, transfixed by the V formation of my wake, pushing away from the propeller in perfect rolls and in differing colours when the sun hit it, and inadvertently slowed down. My lack of concentration meant that at least I wasn't thrown out of the boat. But being pitched forward over the first bench seat, while my fishing rod, water-cooler, esky and swag were thrown over the second seat, was most painful.

The tinnie bounced back off the wood hidden beneath the water and proceeded to go round in slowish circles. Lurching back to my seat I grabbed the steering handle, my legs aching, the banging inside my head feeling like a roadworker with a drill.

Looking quickly around the boat it was clear that nothing, thankfully, had hit the water. Nothing, that was, except my plastic container of worms. For a second or two I thought of all the fish that would be gorging on those limp, wriggling creatures and the irony of it all. Fittingly, perhaps, the only time the bait was to be eaten was when there was no hook attached.

Seeing blood oozing from a grazed leg made me think less about the worms and more about my well-being. I made for shore where there was no sandbar, just a muddy bank with trees. The boat needed to be checked for damage, as it wouldn't do to sink, and I needed to collect my thoughts. Luckily, this was the first mishap of the trip. Well, that was apart from a blown head gasket in the ute and a couple of flat tyres when driving through a forest across spiky sticks of wood. And the water pump that disintegrated near Cobram. Admittedly, I hadn't been on the water all the way but, nevertheless, my record with machinery of any kind was not good.

I was particularly lucky not to have hit a snag before now. The gangs of men who 'snagged' the river to make the passage safer for riverboats had obviously not been here. Their job was not one that lasted long, as just as many trees fell in as were taken out. These days no one is allowed to remove snags at all, even those that have fallen in recently, as they are all considered precious habitat for fish and other creatures of the water.

An hour later, after rearranging the load in the tinnie and sticking my hat back on, cleaning my sunglasses so the scratches didn't obscure my vision too much and, circumspectly, pulling away from the bank, I wish they'd removed at least one.

One thing concerned me. Why did the river do that to me? After all, we had such a good relationship. Perhaps it was just showing me who was in charge; to make sure I kept my eyes open and concentrated. Fair enough, but the message could have been a bit more subtle.

The voyage to Waikerie was uneventful, though a lot more careful than usual.

Built along cliffs and at the edge of a seemingly endless floodplain, Waikerie was another of the communistic style settlements thrust upon people by the government. At least it had a reasonable name. In the local Aboriginal language Waikerie meant 'place of many wings' due to the incredible amount of ibis, pelicans and other soaring birds. Aborigines had named the place well, as the bird life was not only vast but also unavoidable.

A number of the people in Waikerie's original settlement didn't want to work as a collective. Instead, they headed off downstream to places such as Ramco and Holder and set up on their own. They succeeded where the others had failed. Capitalism had won again. After the collapse of the settlement the government took over the whole place and after World War I, like many other such places, it became a soldier settlement.

While loading the tinnie near the Waikerie jetty, and as excess water drained from the plughole, I checked it out for anything that could become a hole. There had been no leaks but I wasn't about to take any chances. The inspection revealed one large dent and scratch marks that ran for about a metre behind the dent—nothing significant. The shock to the system had been the worst thing.

My plan had been to take the boat all the way to Morgan, but my enthusiasm had waned. Instead I retreated and drove home.

Midsummer

Morgan to Mannum

With the tinnie in tow, inspected and ready for more, I drove back to Morgan through the desolate mallee country. As usual at this time of year the land was hot, dry and unyielding. On both sides of the road were dense forests of mallee trees, unfolding like cupped hands from the ground, with only sparse leaves on the end of their twisted, creamy-grey branches. Strips of bark hung down like brown ribbons. Behind them were bare paddocks where the hot northerly winds whipped across the saltbush and where sheep were grateful for whatever they found to eat.

Closer to my destination the country opened up into plains. Once there were trees and lush pastures behind the cliffs along the river, but they disappeared when the white man came with sheep, rabbits and woodcutters. There was a brutal beauty about the land. Then, when I saw the Murray and crossed the river on the ferry into Morgan, everything was once again serene.

Morgan is where the Murray makes a dramatic left-hand turn and heads towards the sea. Folklore suggested the river had travelled westward until it found the best place on earth and, content, then headed directly for the ocean. Others say it decided to head south because there was nothing for it here but flies, sand and rocks. In fact, fault lines had caused the river to go south; it had diverted when the Morgan Plate had risen and started to head towards the sea. If it hadn't, then it is estimated the Murray would have ended at the other side of the Mount Lofty ranges.

Geographically, the North-West Bend, where the river turns and high limestone cliffs rise imperiously on one side, was the extremity of the inland sea that once occupied much of the country. Riverboat captains called it the Great Bend or the Great Elbow.

When the railway arrived in 1878, Morgan, originally called North-West Bend, was the second biggest port in South Australia after Port Adelaide. Sensibly, the town was built on top of the cliffs away from floods. Although its finest hours had long gone there were still plenty of reminders of how the town had once looked.

Even with no more than a lone drinker, the two pubs on opposite corners of the main street were the best indicators of financial success. At the other end of the street, the huge sandstone warehouse once occupied by A.H. Landseer, then the largest shipping and trading company on the Murray, provided further proof of how big and important Morgan had once been.

A few creaking doors up from the pubs, a curiosity shop was full of customers. Stacked in reasonable order in cases or on shelves were old books, antiques, a collection of tools, paintings and other odds and ends to tempt tourists and visitors.

On display in the back room was a collection of patchwork quilts created by the mother of the shop owner. The woman had lived in Morgan most of her life and within two minutes had regaled me with stories about her mother's talent with needle and thread. She also informed me that her mum had still played tenpin bowls three times a week up until her death at ninety-four.

Near the river was the morgue, a cool, stone building where the bodies of those who died along the river were kept until their burial. The PS *Mayflower* was moored along from the morgue. The elegantly restored paddle-steamer was built in Echuca for a West Indian man, Daniel Alexander, or 'Black Alex', as he was known. A gigantic man, said to be the only black man ever to own a paddlewheeler, Black Alex's strength was legendary; he could, it was claimed, lift half a tonne quite easily. He was also reputed to be the best talker and swearer along the river.

Black Alex used his boat for collecting the many discarded bottles along the river but, despite those hard-drinking days, he couldn't collect enough bottles to support the bank payments. The *Mayflower* was seized for debt recovery of £36, but Black Alex stole his boat back and headed upstream. The authorities chased him up the Darling, catching him at Wentworth. A huge fight ensued but Black Alex got away again and was eventually apprehended at Swan Hill after another fight, in which iron bars and chains were used.

The *Mayflower*'s next owner was a bloke who used the shallow draft to get into the places where other boats couldn't go. This advantage meant the rates he charged for freight were quite exorbitant, leading to his nickname of 'Pirate'.

Sitting quite calmly in the water now, the *Mayflower* looked anything but concerned about her history.

Making my way along the old railway line, past the station-master's ticket office and the goods shed, I sat on the wharf high above the river and could almost hear the echoes of the wharfies' cries as they plunged from the tops of the cranes into the water. When river trade was at its peak and men unloaded the steamers by hand, it was believed that the higher the place from which he jumped, the braver the man. Those who managed the feat could drink on the escapade for life, but some came to grief and broke legs, ribs and, on the odd occasion, necks. But that was in the days when safety issues were unimportant, when men took risks and enjoyed them; when it was simply fun to be a daredevil. When the river was high the jumping distance wasn't great, but if the river was low then it could be the height of the crane plus the ten metres of the wharf and then a few more into water that was not very deep.

The wharf was once 160 metres long, and had five water hydraulic cranes worked by a complex mass of pipes, gearing and drive shafts connected to a steam boiler. A network of ladders and stairs and decking was constructed below the top of the wharf so steamers could be unloaded whatever the level of the river. Shifts of up to forty men worked around the clock. Steamers from along the Darling and the Murray would be lined up for a kilometre during the busy times and five or six trains a day would pull into the wharf, loading goods for the outback stations and wool to be taken to Adelaide. Morgan was also the hub from which fruit from the Riverland district could be shipped to Adelaide. That continued until Victoria extended its railway to Mildura, after which the river trade to Adelaide died a slow painful death.

Looked at from water level in the tinnie on my way to the bend a short distance upstream, the wharf was even more imposing, even though it was now just 60 metres long. I stroked the red gum timber legs and tried to put my arms around one; they barely reached halfway. The smell and feel of the wood spoke eloquently of the memories soaked inside. Bolts that would have once been shiny and new were rusted and corroded but still securely in place.

The river water swirled around the pylons as the boat moved away. Watching the water carefully and only travelling slowly, determined not to suffer a repeat of my mishap near Waikerie, I soon came upon a pumping station that seemed almost to be carved into the cliffs. A huge brick building, it had pipes going in all directions and a large security fence surrounding it. Nearby, amongst lovely lawns and gardens and with an extraordinary view, sat what was presumably the pumping station boss's house. This was the beginning of the pipeline that made its way across the desert to Whyalla, a lifeline from the river for a community 350 kilometres away. Most of Adelaide's water came from Morgan and Mannum, together with around 90 per cent of the rest of the state's water, pumped to places as diverse as Keith, Port Pirie, Port Augusta, the Yorke Peninsula and Woomera.

Contemplating the amount of water and the pressure needed to send water that distance continuously was difficult, as was thinking about salt. Salt has always reached the river because of saline groundwater; however, over the last forty years levels have risen because of irrigation, land clearance and drainage. The state of salinity in the Murray is generally gauged by levels recorded at Morgan. The aim is to keep it below 800 EC units, the level at which the World Health Organisation says that water is no longer potable.

Concerns about salt and water pressure were soon left behind as the river eased around a bend and the rusting ribs of the barge *Crowie* came into view. Reputed to be the biggest barge on the river, the *Crowie* was built in 1911 and had sunk where it was moored in 1946. From under the shade of the gum trees on the opposite bank, what remained of the *Crowie* was easier to see. Saplings and weeds grew around the decaying hulk. Birds landed and took off with impunity. Sadly, the *Crowie* would eventually rust completely away, leaving the rushes and the trees to grow unhindered.

Parked in the rough camping ground a hundred metres away was a yellow bus—named, unsurprisingly, 'Old Yella'— with Western Australian licence plates. Converted into a mobile home, the bus had curtains on the windows, and even though the door was open no one was inside. As I was about to leave the owner appeared and walked straight past me. A forlorn, elderly figure wearing only shorts and thongs and with skin like a deflated balloon hanging off his brown torso, he wasn't in the mood for conversation.

'Following the river?' I inquired.

'Not really,' came the reply as he kept on walking. 'Just campin' here for a few nights cos I like it.'

'From the west?' I asked as he walked on.

'Nah,' he called over his shoulder. 'I send 'em the money and they send me the rego.'

He stopped at the doorway to the bus, smiled at me, and with two quick steps he was gone and the door was closed. When I went past in the tinnie five minutes later he was standing on the bank waving.

After rounding another huge bend, the ferry at Cadell came into view. Cadell, a small town named after the pioneer of the riverboats, was another of the irrigation settlements granted to soldiers after World War I. It was also home to a training centre, where selected prisoners could work a farm as part of their rehabilitation. Not wanting anyone to mistake me for a crook or an escaped convict, I headed back to Morgan, sweeping around the great bend as the old steamers used to do, and at about the same pace.

After a slow 22 kilometres from Morgan, I reached Murbko in the late afternoon with the sun still hot, pulling in just downstream from a row of shacks. There were many of these buildings around these parts. During the Depression homeless or people fallen on hard times were allowed to live in shanties they'd erected on the banks of the river. When these people progressed to more permanent accommodation, their patch of the river was taken over by other, less needy people. Holiday shacks are now prevalent all along this stretch of the Murray. Of course, apart from sewage, all their waste ends up in the river.

There were too many holiday makers for me at Murbko and there would be just as many at Blanchetown, the next big town along the river, so my camp for the night was between the two at Roonka, a short distance downstream from McBean's Pound. This was one of the first places mooted as a railway crossing on the Murray but Lachlan McBean, who owned Roonka Roonka station, didn't want his stock disturbed by trains or his land used for anything else, so the railway went elsewhere.

Roonka, an Aboriginal word for the grubs of moths found in tree roots, is one of the country's most important archaeological sites. A cemetery was discovered here containing a substantial number of skeletons. Humans had camped here almost twenty thousand years before; the earliest burials were between four thousand and seven thousand years ago.

Bodies at Roonka were buried in a curious fashion. Adult bodies were either upright or bent over, while some graves contained food, bone awls and stone artifacts. Some bodies were elaborately clad in jewellery and animal skins secured with bone pins, others were accompanied by an infant. Graves hinted at death by childbirth, death by genetic abnormality, judicial executions and death through disease and spearing. The skeleton of one young woman revealed that she was unable to give birth to her child—the child's skull was found, partly emerged, at the narrow pelvic opening. Her predicament may have ended with a mercy blow to the head, as her skull was fractured.

One grave held the body of a child resting on the left arm of the skeleton of a strong man and, according to the experts, was the most striking and elaborate tomb unearthed in Australia. It recorded the first instance of Aboriginal crowning of the dead.

Perhaps it was my latent fascination with ghosts and history, but something told me that despite any noises in the night or any apparitions that might appear, the river and its memories would keep me safe here.

The lock and weir at Blanchetown was the first one built on the Murray. Prior to that the old riverboat skippers had huge problems navigating through the sandbars, reefs and other places where the water was shallow. When the river was low they were often left stranded for weeks. The lock solved the problem but, ironically, not long after it was completed the river trade died away.

Opposite the entrance to the lock was a tiny stone church bearing a sign informing churchgoers that services were only held once a month. Alongside the church was the lock keeper's house. As well as a garden full of concrete statues, it had a swing set up near the fence upon which a hessian-stuffed trio of mother, father and child swung happily. Beside the swing stood a bike with the front wheel removed, replaced by the blades of a push mower, an excellent combination of exercise and practicality for the gardens of the lock.

The lock keeper, Ron Simpfendorfer, told me he was not allowed to keep the bike on the lock premises for fear of someone jumping on it and falling off. 'Occupational Health and Safety implications, y'know.'

Ron had been the lock keeper for eleven years and had, from my observation, one of the best jobs in the world. He agreed, before smiling and advising me of the difference between the lock keeper and the lock master; the lock keeper did all the work after the lock master gave the orders. At the time of our conversation the lock master was nowhere to be seen.

Each day Ron sat in his office and waited for boats to come along. His job description, apart from keeping the surrounds tidy and making sure everything worked well, was to put river traffic through the lock and to keep the weir levels at the correct heights. This meant that, depending on the amount coming down the river, water went over the weir twenty-four hours a day. Otherwise, Ron explained, everything would back up and flood.

Some river craft simply turned up at the lock and had to wait, but the better organised rang ahead or gave a couple of blasts on their whistle and Ron would have the gates open and ready for them when they arrived.

'Most people are good and fairly patient but some are a bit demanding,' said Ron in an apparent understatement. 'The best are the first-timers who can make life a bit interesting for themselves.'

The river had always meant a lot to Ron but since he had been working at the lock, 'sitting here all the time watching it flow past, reckon I'd bleed water now.' He said this was the best job he'd ever had and 'it's the best one I could ever have'.

At the lower side of the lock hundreds of pelicans sat and waited patiently for fish to swim by. From his vantage point in the office, Ron watched the show of nature regularly and had noticed the pelicans sometimes weren't as nice and graceful as they appeared. When one of the three or four brave shags managed to snare a fish they were besieged by pelicans that would fight them for it, occasionally grabbing the shag by the neck and holding them under the water until they either let go or drowned.

Ron had to walk to the other side of the weir to check out a few things on his demanding schedule so my only companions for a while were pelicans. Ten minutes later, as none had seized any fish, I left. Perhaps my own bad luck with fish was rubbing off.

I soon left Ron and Blanchetown behind and headed to the area where the explorer Edward Eyre once lived. In 1841 Eyre was granted the title of Protector of Aborigines and Special Magistrate, based at Moorunde in the area between Blanchetown and Swan Reach.

During this time attacks on overlanders bringing stock from outback New South Wales to Adelaide had people in fear for their lives. (Of course the reprisals of the white man were as bad as the attacks.) As a result, at the time of Eyre's appointment there were no permanent settlers on the river between Overland Corner and Wellington, where the river enters Lake Alexandrina.

Eyre put an end to all that. Clearly a man with a gentle and persuasive touch, shortly after he took up his post he managed to pacify the local tribes without the need for guns. In three years he brought harmony between the cultures along the river.

Eyre was also one of the first to try irrigation and spent a fortune on his project. He built a couple of dams that collapsed during what was known as the Gundagai Floods. Although Gundagai was nowhere near the Murray, its name was used as, before the locks were built, the tributary or river from where the floods originated was identified by the colour of the water and named accordingly.

Eyre returned to England in 1843 and the Aborigines at Moorunde suffered. When he left, rations were supplied for four hundred Aborigines. By 1864 there were only two hundred. Twenty years later there were none. European diseases of small-pox and the like swept along the river, destroying all those who had no in-built generational immunity.

The tinnie almost flew across the top of the water as I powered on towards Mannum. Three days was all that was left before work and the monotony of everyday life recalled me. The river hereabouts was treacherous and my focus was constantly on the sandbars, rocks and other hazards the *Murray River Pilot* warned me about. At the side of the river were lagoons of varying shapes and sizes, all fed by the river and all a navigational problem in the old days for riverboat captains when the river was in flood.

The river around Swan Reach is an example of just how slow it moves. Even though it is still over 140 river kilometres from Lake Alexandrina, it is only .75 of a metre above sea level. Stopping briefly to replenish my water container, I walked up the slight hill to the local hotel that was once the original Swan Reach homestead, the largest station in the area. Set on top of the cliffs, the hotel has sweeping views over the river and surrounding area.

The 1956 floods had devastated Swan Reach. Normally the river at Morgan flows at about 113 cubic metres per day, but during the floods of 1956 that figure rose to over 3900. And while Morgan was set on a cliff, most of Swan Reach wasn't and the water engulfed the town, washing away most of the businesses in the main street. But, being peopled with hardy and optimistic folk, the town was quickly rebuilt.

Back on the water, my attention turned to keeping the boat speed constant, as it created a breeze that dried the sweat on my face, preventing it from dripping into the sunscreen and making a congealed mess. My facial comfort sorted, I turned my attention back to the river. At Big Bend, not only did the river bend turn in the shape of a horseshoe, the tallest cliffs on the Murray rose above me. The cliffs around Nildottie were shorter but the shade provided by them also helped with the heat as I zipped past.

This stretch of the river is rich with archaeological sites. Barely 60 kilometres from Roonka is Devon Downs, which holds the Ngaut Ngaut Conservation Park, site of another important Australian discovery. In the 1930s, the station's owner came across a skeleton in the rocks nearby. Anthropologist Norman Tindale was quickly on the scene, and he declared the boy to have been around twelve years of age when he died. Tribes known as the Murrayians, who came to live on the river about seven thousand years previously, had probably killed him. To their amazement the anthropologists discovered the boy was a negrito, a relative of the Tasmanian Aborigines who, until then, were considered to have been a separate race.

The cliffs in this stretch of the river were relatively new, only 17 000 years old, and were carved after the Ice Age ended. Beforehand, sea levels were low with temperate rainforests and metres of water trying to find its way down to sea level. When the Ice Age finished and sea levels rose, the land was left with the big gorge and a low flat river.

I set up camp opposite the cliffs in a clearing on the land between the river and a lagoon, and, as usual, threw in a line— though I knew what that meant. Plenty of fish would have swum past if there were no line in the water but because *my* line was there, they wouldn't. I knew there would be no fish, but hope springs eternal and all that.

That night, the twin menaces of mosquitoes and heat, combined with the noise that came from argumentative possums, made sleep difficult. When it did creep up the shadowy appearance of the cliffs in the moonlight made me want to keep my eyes open. The top of the cliffs was one of the central meeting places for Aboriginal tribes from the area. They'd trade goods here, and conduct important tribal ceremonies. They'd settle disputes and feast on fish and duck and kangaroo. They'd paint themselves and dance and celebrate. Long before the Tudor kings, long before William the Conqueror, long before the Pharaohs built their pyramids, these tribes were here bartering and talking.

And, all the while, the river had slid silently past.

Late summer

Mannum to Wellington

Backing the tinnie down to the water at Mannum in 40-degree heat caused rivulets of sweat to run into my eyes. Masses of flies were there to help me unload and waving them away, wiping my eyes and mooring the boat all at once proved rather difficult.

Overcoming those small but annoying obstacles didn't take long and, after losing my hat in the water a couple of times, I slipped out into the middle of the river, heading upstream to see the things I'd missed when driving into town.

Earlier I'd been across the river and back again on the two ferries, talking to both ferrymen about what to look out for. One said 'mad bastards in speedboats', the other said 'every-thing'. The second was the one with sound advice. He also told me that ferrymen at Mannum worked seven-day rotations of twelve-hour shifts with around seventy-two crossings a shift.

Good rains in the catchment areas over the last few months had flushed the river and it showed. The river was higher than it had been for some time and the water appeared cleaner. No doubt the South Australians approved. This was how it should be all the time, said the man who had launched his expensive craft next to me.

Water authorities had even let an environmental flow into the Barmah Forest—the biggest, it was reported, in Australia's history. Col Walker would have been pleased, as would the birds, animals, fish, turtles and other reptiles. If they'd left it much longer the wildlife population could have been decimated, but now they could breed happily. For the first time in thirty years, egrets were building nests and ibis and pelicans were plentiful. Another good thing about the flood was that 80 per cent of the water in the forest would be returned to the Murray, cleaner and richer in nutrients.

However, the man with the humiliatingly big boat said it was still noticeable that people were wasting water. 'Why can't they get it through their thick heads that there is only so much of it around? Why can't people be less greedy?'

With a deep-throated gurgle his boat lurched forward and then settled in the water. 'Proper regulation is what we need; proper control from everyone—irrigators like me, included— then we'll be okay.' He revved the engine and took off, leaving a streak of oil swirling on the surface and a wake that wobbled the small boats moored nearby.

Of all the craft on the river here, the tinnie was by far the most ordinary. Even the smallest fishing boats were larger and more elaborate. Houseboats of all shapes and sizes lined the banks together with launches both old and wooden and the more modern steel-built variety. Those awaiting repairs were pulled out of the water on slipways while a couple languished near the bank, partly submerged. On the opposite side of the river to the town, some were moored in front of holiday houses built on stilts. Willow trees filled every spare space.

This time there were no fallen trees or snags to worry about and the water was deep enough for me to motor along easily and safely at a decent speed. Not too fast, mind you, I didn't want to be guilty of making waves.

The birthplace of paddle-steamers, Noa No Landing was only five kilometres into the trip but Pellaring Reach, a part of the river exposed to winds from every direction, was my initial destination. Even Captain Sturt found the going too rough here and put ashore for a few days until the weather calmed down. Now it was shimmering in the heat, the glare from the water harsh.

This was a plain section of the river; there were no cliffs, just normal banks with lakes and lagoons further back. Stone Wall, at the end of Pellaring Reach, had a reputation as one of the best known fishing reaches in the old days so, despite having promised never to torment myself again, I tied up and settled down to find out if the story was true.

After attaching one of the decent-sized worms that the garage attendant in Mannum assured me were the best on the river, the line snaked out and landed with a distinct 'thunk' just where the fish were most likely to be. The garage man was a local and so couldn't be doubted, but I had a shrimp net handy in order to offer the fish a bit more choice. If all else failed, I still had the cheese in the esky. Once the line was in place and the rod fixed in the rod-holder riveted to the side of the tinnie, the only thing left to do was sit in the heat, watch and wait.

An hour later and without a bite the heat was becoming unbearable. Sitting in a boat with no shade and no breeze is not the easiest thing to do. The garage man had advised me that the best way to get one of those elusive fish was to troll a lure out the back of the boat. I'd already tried that but, after retrieving the line and hauling in the empty shrimp net, I slowly headed off, this time sporting a brand-new bright red stump-jump lure capable of enticing the fish from about four metres below the surface.

Around almost every bend were more holiday shacks and, in places, what seemed like almost one continuous willow. A couple of kids, unperturbed by the heat, were playing cricket on the grass verge in front of a row of shacks opposite the cliffs at Coolcha, just up from Piggy Flat lagoon. They stopped their game as they heard my motor, waved and called out, so I pulled in.

The shady tree serving as their wicket was also welcome shade and as they resumed their game their father explained that he had inherited the shack from his father who had, in turn, inherited it from his. He wasn't sure how it all came about but said that he didn't mind it being old; it fitted in with the feel of the river.

The family came from Adelaide most weekends during the summer and didn't own a boat, just a couple of canoes. He reckoned that his body switched off when he came here, and that the less there was to distract them the more they could see and appreciate what was around them. 'We don't need a boat or TV or radio; we just need us and the silence after a week or so in the city.'

Although he knew that as the children grew older their time would be taken up by sport or studies and these weekends would become fewer, it was good while it lasted. 'And when they have grown and they come here by themselves they'll remember these days. It's important to have that continuity, that link with the past.'

After watching a rather long brown snake wriggle across the river in front of me, thoughts of catching fish by trolling disappeared. What would happen if I accidentally caught one of the many snakes around and pulled it into the tinnie? Or worse still, what if one of them decided to share the water with me while I was swimming?

By the time Chucka Bend came up, I decided to turn back, going a little faster to create a cooling breeze and to make sure snakes stayed well clear. The bend was named after a bloke called Charlie Craven who had camped nearby and was thrown from his horse into the water. Charlie was also said to have put a few shots into the Bogan Hotel in Mannum while practising with a pistol. To escape arrest he stayed ahead of the police during a wild buggy ride across the flats before swimming the river on his horse and heading home.

After another hour of shacks, cliffs and the river heat I reached Walker's Flat. The cliffs here were renowned for their spectacular colour more than for their height. In the 1920s a petrified shark twenty million years old was found in one of the cliffs.

This was where the Manunka people lived, and Ginny Christmas was their queen. Ginny was the mother of Henry Mason, the leader of the last Aborigines at Mannum to live tribally. In the 1930s their campsite in the town was overrun by the urban sprawl and they moved to a mission near Swan Reach. For thousands of years their people had lived on the food from the river and the land, but in the mission everything they did was controlled.

Midafternoon was the hottest part of the day but the sun, thankfully, was beginning its decline. Running the risk of a miscreant snag materialising, I headed back downstream, keeping to the side of the river where the cliffs made it shady.

Back at Noa No landing, where the whole story of paddle-steamers began, and away from the protection of the cliffs, it was even hotter than the forecast 42 degrees. After tying up to one of the many willows I waded the few steps to the bank and walked across to a cairn. The brass plaque indicated that this was the spot where William Randell and his brothers, Thomas and Elliott, finished assembling the *Mary Ann*, and where in February 1852 it was launched.

Randell had used timber from the family mill 50 kilometres away at Gumeracha in the Mount Lofty Ranges before he and his brothers dragged the half-built vessel across country to complete the task near the river. The process took almost a year but after the square boiler was connected to the paddlewheels, the *Mary Ann* headed off to Goolwa, where Randell had discussions with the customs department after loading stores for the Victorian goldfields.

After reading the plaque, and ignoring the risk posed by wriggling reptiles, I dropped my hat on the ground, removed my sweat-stained shirt, and plunged headlong into the water.

There is that wonderful moment when, holding your breath, you leave the air and dive into the water, when you are engulfed by the exquisite feeling of quiet before exploding through the surface back into the real world. An instant cool washed over me and, with the river holding me gently, I swam further out, my body's temperature decreasing with every stroke.

Randell and his brothers must have done this many times. They may even have leapt with a yell from the decks or the superstructure while the boat floated that first time; an intimate celebration of the sheer joy of achievement.

On returning from his first voyage Randell transferred his business to Mannum, where he built the wharf, goods shed and a cottage. As the river trade grew the town grew with it.

Twenty years later Randell journeyed to Milang on the other side of Lake Alexandrina and towed a floating dry dock back to Mannum to service the growing number of paddle-steamers on the river. The excavation of the riverbank was successful, as was getting the dock in place, but when the water was pumped out the dock started to rise, so Randell drove a number of large wooden piles through it to ensure it stayed in place. After these slight modifications the dock served the river industry for many years then fell into disrepair before being restored to become a permanent fixture in what was now the Mannum Heritage Centre.

The river end of the dock had had a permanent wall put in place when it was found the dock door couldn't be sealed. When working properly, the door dropped down into the river and the boat going into the dock would float over the top. Steam winches would then haul the door back up and the water was pumped out.

The original red gum timber remained and, although still solid, had worn considerably. Pylons on the angled sides had rotted away, as had the side shoring. Steel rollers that helped the craft slip in on the bottom of the lock were rusty and decaying. Twisted rusty bolts that had once held everything together were bent at obscure angles all along the timber.

A workman watched me from a distance. In the 1980s Dave had taken part in digging dirt out of the dock. He was also the man who made sure there was enough wood for the PS *Marion*, the paddle-steamer tied up at the wharf.

The last wood-fired, steam-driven, passenger-carrying steamer on the river, the *Marion* spent her first years as a working boat, then was turned into a boarding house. Now she was part of the museum, but still took passengers on trips up the Murray. Locals had contributed over 100 000 working hours to bring her back to running condition.

One of the *Marion*'s cargos in the late 1800s was machinery designed and built by the Shearer brothers, who invented Australia's famous stump-jump plough. The Shearers' factory began as the Mannum blacksmith's shop where, as well as inventing their plough, the brothers forged ploughshares that revolutionised the farming industry in the mallee. For fifty years paddleboats loaded their machinery from Shearer's Wharf and took it as far as the water would carry them. John Shearer's motto was 'work is life; idleness is death'.

In the museum next to the dry dock were pictures of the *Marion* and other boats loading and unloading. A special section on the 1956 floods showed the devastating effect the floods had on the main street of the town, which was under water up to the roofs of many buildings.

Those towards the top of the hill were safe, those halfway down sustained some damage, while buildings at the base of the hill were destroyed, despite the best efforts of local sandbaggers. It took months for the water to recede. Dave said there could never be another flood like it. Johnny Gurr at Renmark would have disagreed.

Heading up the main street for supplies, I ducked into what appeared to be one of the oldest buildings in town. Through a couple of rooms stocked with books, souvenirs and paintings was an outdoor café. What could be termed as junk was piled onto a number of tables. I was the sole customer and asked the woman who served me if she was having a garage sale. Rose Williams replied that her husband, Rod, had recently died and she needed to get rid of some stuff.

Her husband, she told me, had been an enthusiastic river historian and he had written extensively about the Murray. One of his favourite stories, according to Rose, was that of Swedish-born J.G. Arnold, who replaced William Randell as 'king of the river'. Arnold bought Randell's dockyard and set about creating an empire, with boats all along the river system and an exporting business based in Victor Harbor. On one trip he came across a sick stockman whom he took on board. The man died, even though they made a full-speed dash to Blanchetown. Arnold continued on to Mannum, where he asked the local JP to sign the necessary papers to give the man a decent burial. The JP refused, whereupon Arnold told his crew to throw the body into the river as he had more important things to do than argue with a bureaucrat. The JP quickly changed his mind.

Rose showed me a book of her husband's that told the story of how willow trees came to be along this stretch of the river. The original three hundred came from England on sailing ships in the early 1800s. All two metres high, they were stuck into potatoes to keep them moist. Despite the long journey, 290 of them survived and were planted between Mannum and Murray Bridge. Then, in 1902, eight hundred more arrived, this time about four metres high. Folklore had it that the first was planted at Moorunde and was a cutting from the tree planted at Napoleon Bonaparte's grave.

At the Mary Ann Reserve, a grassed parkland alongside the river, the largest boat ever to ply the river was pulling alongside. A purpose-built sternwheeler, the MV *Murray Princess* was based at Mannum and went both up and downstream with trips ranging from a couple of days to a week.

The skipper, Ray Weedon, was the man charged with navigating this huge vessel. The Murray had been the major part of Ray's life for over half of his fifty-six years. After building and hiring small boats then progressing to larger replica paddleboats, Ray felt sure he had Murray water in his veins. For years he had worked in the Goolwa shipyards, building his boat, the *Lady Mannum*. A few years later, in 1985, after selling the boat to a man in Queensland, he took it out of the Murray Mouth and sailed it up to the Gold Coast. Ray had partially retired before returning as Senior Ships Master and now had the pleasure of taking the *Princess* along the river.

The wheelhouse on the *Princess* was high above the water, almost like a small seagoing ship. It stretched the full width of the boat, and boasted polished brass and wood in abundance. This was where Ray navigated, in much the same way as the old riverboat captains had. Even though the *Princess* carried depth sounders, the water was so shallow that most of the time they couldn't be read. More importantly, they needed to know what was ahead of them. The charts Ray used weren't much different from those used by the old skippers 150 years before. 'We've made our own alterations, adjusted them here and there, but essentially they're the same.'

The charts were kept in a large folder, page by page, reach by reach. Notations were made where perhaps an old tree once hung over the river but had since fallen in, so it was now marked as a snag. A particular-shaped tree would be an indication of a pile of rocks and perhaps some smaller trees would point to a new channel. Then there were sandbars that had shifted and notes about where Ray needed the *Princess* close to the bank or where differ-ent hazards could be seen at different river heights. Their draft was 1.1 metres and in some places the river was only 1.6 metres deep, so they 'knocked a few lumps off the bottom as we go'.

The size of the *Princess* made navigation difficult. Although it was some 60 metres long, it was the breadth that was the biggest problem. Making their way around the bends where the river was very narrow or through channels in sandbars was easier said than done. Smaller boats with a couple of metres of depth could skip through them with no problems, but to the *Princess* it was like a valley between two sandhills; the middle bit was deep enough but the sides were very shallow. Ray laughed. 'We go along with a list as we scrape and slide the hull along the sand; lots of groaning and bumping.'

With a few waves of his hand and shimmers of his body Ray explained how the *Princess* moved along the water. 'With a flat-bottomed boat you end up sliding sideways a lot of the time and when you are coming down to a corner you turn the wheel and the three big rudders work well; the boat responds but it doesn't stop.'

He said that with no keel the boat keeps sliding sideways. 'You have to anticipate when to turn, sometimes you have to start turning up to a hundred metres before the bend, and although it looks as if you are going to run into the bank, in effect you go past and power the boat out of it with opposite lock, like a rally car.'

Near the bow of the *Princess* was a large pole that was used as a crane to swing out and lift stores onto the boat and that was used as a steering pole just as it was done in the old days. Given the huge length of the *Princess*, the pole's function was to let Ray know what was happening behind him. 'I use it to be aware of the whole boat. If the pole's on an angle then my stern will be close to the bank. I extend the pole through the vessel and then I know where the stern is the whole time.'

A wind indicator on the pole was important, as on windy days the superstructure catches wind and the pressure is enormous. 'We have to turn the rudders so as to crab down the river, otherwise being blown against the bank is a distinct possibility. Crabbing hasn't always worked though; a couple of times we've had to winch ourselves off banks. But it's all a big adventure for the passengers.'

As we talked a constant stream of crew members came through the wheelhouse, all of them asking questions. The chef, the cleaners, electricians, deckhands, all had queries for Ray, who simply smiled, gave them the answer and turned back to me.

On each trip he spoke to passengers, telling them about the river's history and about the future, which, he added, needs to be taken a lot more seriously than it currently is. A couple of examples he gave on his talks were that it takes 4500 litres of water to grow $1 worth of rice and that cotton farms were totally out of place on this dry continent. 'I know we have to have economic development and employment and all that, but why can't we grow crops more natural to Australia and more sustainable with the amount of water we have?'

After one of his talks he had a spin doctor from the rice industry ring to say that his figures were wrong. Ray looked up the figures from the CSIRO. They indicated it actually took 8400 litres. He was vindicated but, 'whichever figure is correct, it is still a bloody lot of water.' As for cotton, 'Why can't we grow that up north where they have an abundance of water?'

According to Ray, irrigation is all about wealth creation, with no thought—or not much—given to sustainability. 'In a hundred years the water will be gone—governments must just *do* something; I've been listening to people talk for twenty-five years or more.'

He apologised for getting carried away. 'I'm spreading the gospel, I bash everyone I can, but you get that way about the river . . . There are places along the river I've walked into and had the same feeling as when I walk into a cathedral or a war memorial. But that feeling is being lost in places.'

Ray said he still went searching for those places, for that solace and the oneness you find. We both knew the places were still there. He looked out from the wheelhouse window. 'I couldn't ever give any of this away. The river is life; it's *my* life.'

Passing the *Princess* in the tinnie on my way downstream made me feel like a small shrimp on the back of a huge old cod. I could see Ray in the wheelhouse answering more questions while the crew lumped passenger's bags on board. How would the visitors respond to Ray on this trip? Hopefully they would all return somewhat more enlightened than when they left.

The man with the cricket-playing kids at Pellaring Reach had said that 'the world had gone mad' with shacks. He had a point. There were shacks, shacks and more shacks. Most of them were on crown land—which went unchecked—and most had signs impertinently telling people to keep going and not to tie up.

At Ponde, the place they called the Water of the Great Murray Cod, I tried to find a sense of the fish story. Huge cod up to 50 kilos were caught in these waters long after they'd disappeared from other places in the river, so perhaps Ngurunderi had passed this way after all. Would these waters relinquish a cod for me? I didn't waste time finding out; I knew I was destined never to be fulfilled as far as fishing was concerned. After another four hours on the water I went under two bridges, one for rail, the other for vehicles.

Murray Bridge was first known as Edward's Crossing after the first white settler who took his stock across the river. When George Edwards died three years after arriving his wife opened a boarding house at the crossing to provide for herself and her eight children. Some also knew the place as Turn Off because overlanders would either cross the river and continue south or turn towards Adelaide. After Edward's Crossing the town became known as Mobilong, a derivation of the Aboriginal word 'moop pol tha wong', meaning 'haven for birds'. The official name was not gazetted until 1924.

It took nine years from the decision to build the bridge over the Murray to its opening in 1879. As usual, political squabbling was the cause of delays in the construction.

It was said to be the first bridge across the Murray, a claim that would be disputed by the people in Echuca, who knew that Henry Hopwood had a pontoon bridge in place twenty years before that. There were also bridges at Albury and Wahgunyah which would lay claim to have been built earlier.

Seven years after it was opened, the railway came to the bridge. Gates at each end stopped the road traffic until after the train had crossed. The separate railway bridge was built fifty years later.

The town grew dramatically after the bridge opened, taking over the bulk of the cargo from Mannum to Goolwa. Most produce came there for transportation to Adelaide and Melbourne. It was also a place where dairy farms were visited by scows similar to the one my friend with the Murray River flags had had, transporting milk to the dairy factories in Murray Bridge.

William Randell's son Richard retired from life on the river here, living in his boat *Murrundi*. Soon enough the boat sank, but Richard had the deckhouse removed to the shore and lived there until his death. On the wharf close to where Randell and many other captains had tied up was a curious brown-coloured steel-hulled replica of a paddle-steamer.

The PS *Madam Jade* had a number of handwritten signs attached to various parts of the superstructure. The main one announced it as a trading boat, the only one still on the Murray. While most paddle-steamers had ferried freight and produce up and down the rivers, there had been many trading boats plying the river selling goods to townsfolk and those from further inland who came down to the river whenever a boat arrived. As outback hawkers traded from horse and wagon, or even from camel trains, these were the hawkers of the river system.

A beeping sound on the small gangplank announced my arrival on board. Two short staircases on the stern led to the top cabin, but there was no one inside. A noise or two came from below and soon a woman appeared.

Kath Bentley, a short woman with greying hair, introduced herself, and I realised she was the person who had written *River of Islands*, my guide between the Hume Dam and Yarrawonga. Sitting at her usual place on a comfortable seat at the flywire door, her memories of the guide's creation returned. 'That's a long story.'

With her late husband Leon, Kath had spent many years on the river, beginning when she answered an advertisement placed in a Melbourne magazine, *Parents Without Partners*, Leon wanted someone to accompany him on a few weeks' holiday to the river. Kath applied, 'got the job', and so began their love affair with each other and the Murray.

One trip led to another and it wasn't long before they planned a journey from the Hume Dam to Yarrawonga. The couple looked for charts to help guide them but there were none. So they produced their own, the only charts available now for that part of the river. Leon drew the outline of the river to scale on a continuous roll, as the old charts were, while Kath marked everything they saw. I was pleased when Kath said they had looked at the river from both directions as 'the river looks entirely different going from the other way'.

Leon had built a number of boats, including a trailer-sailer in which the couple eventually sailed down various parts of the river, masts and sails up, gathering whatever breeze there was. As property along the top end of the river was extremely expensive, they gave up their jobs in Melbourne and bought a cheaper house in Morgan to fulfil their dream of living near the Murray. In 1986 they decided to build a boat big enough to go up and down the river, trading as they went—not exactly the same as in the old days, but with the same intention.

Leon started building the *Madam Jade* in 1987, the first ship built in Morgan for eighty years. In an old creek bed next to the house they had sold to finance the project, the boat gradually took shape. The boat wasn't based on any other vessel in particular, just a collection of ideas from everything they'd seen. Four years later, on 27 September 1991, the *Madam Jade*—23 metres in length, with a draft of just half a metre, weighing 50 tonnes, and named after a pet Dalmatian who had died during construction—cruised upstream to Renmark.

The couple lived in the cabin on the main deck while everything for sale was piled into the room on the top deck. On different shelves and various dressers and tables were old books, collectables, a few old tools, and general odds and ends—a sort of river-bound trash-and-treasure stall. For ten years the couple had sailed up and down the river from Mildura to Goolwa, eking out their existence in river tranquillity.

Leon passed away in 2001 after twenty-five years together, and as it takes two to crew a vessel of that size, Kath had not been able to travel as they once did. After living on board the *Madam Jade* for fifteen years, she planned to sell the boat, and was moored at Murray Bridge while waiting for a buyer. 'I miss Leon dreadfully and being stuck here's not the same,' she said. 'But that's life, I haven't got much choice.'

A self-confessed adventurer, Kath said she loved the river most when she and Leon were out of the towns, out of the commercial areas—when it was just them and the water. 'We didn't mind being on our own; we had each other. Our favourite place was just up from Lock 7.'

Kath bowed her head for a few seconds, then smiled. 'That's where I spread Leon's ashes.'

Apart from dairy farms and banks lined with willows there wasn't much to see between Murray Bridge and Tailem Bend. The origin of the name 'Tailem' had two explanations. The indigenous version was that it came from the word 'thelim', which meant 'bend in the river' in the local language. The other was that it came from 'tail 'em', linked to tailing lambs. I preferred the first.

A grass embankment at a section noticeably devoid of willows was the frontage for the Tailem Bend Riverside Hotel where, at the top of the walkway, the woman behind the bar assured me they never had any trouble with pilferers. I dragged the tinnie half of its length up the bank, bound it to the one willow tree on the bank and lugged my stuff first up the cliff walkway, then up the stairs to my room.

Inside there was an ancient double bed and wardrobe, a cracked sink and a light globe that swung from the end of a cord. The television antenna was draped peculiarly across the door of the wardrobe so as to get the best reception. The room was, as the woman explained, spartan to say the least. There were two saving graces; one was that it was cheap, and the other was that from the window the view of the river was worth a thousand dollars.

Downstairs, after taking a beer onto the verandah, it was easy to see why the woman said the pub was a popular spot. The view from the deck looking back upstream was different from that of most other cliffs on the river. Their views were mainly of bushland, whereas from my vantage point 30 metres high, the whole river plain was laid out. The land spread away, rising and falling with the small hills. The willows looked like Beatles haircuts, big mopped tops of green, while behind them were paddocks, one with freshly baled hay, another with cows all contentedly grazing in the lush green feed, yet another with thick hay waiting to be cut. A cool change was on the way and the dark clouds of an approaching storm mingled with those which were white with a blackish base. Both sat threateningly over the land while the intensity of the wind picked up. Streaks of rain appeared on the horizon as though someone had washed a window badly. The freshening wind caused small white-capped waves to rise on the river, making it appear as though it was flowing quickly, which it wasn't. A houseboat passed below and sounded its claxon-toned horn. Near the small homemade pontoon below the tinnie lay still and quiet, empty and bare, but in no danger.

I left the pub and walked along the street. A few hundred metres away, where the ferry crossed the river, a truck bearing the name 'O'Grady's Contractors', with a large tank on its back, was sucking water from the river through a large dirty hose. O'Grady, presumably, leapt from the back of the truck to check the pump and told me the water was for the wheat silo down the road. Dust from the grain made life uncomfortable for workers in the hot weather, so he took water up and spread it around to lay the dust. A good idea in theory, said O'Grady, but by the time he'd deposited the water and returned with another load, it was dusty again.

O'Grady was nearing retirement age and had lived in Tailem Bend all his life. His grey hair had a bald patch from the top of his neck to the top of his forehead in the same place that some young men have mohawks. 'Poor old thing,' he said, looking at the Murray as the pump slurped the water into the tank. 'They expect it to do wonders.'

Many places in the state received water from this part of the river. Although most of it was pumped from Mannum and Morgan there was a refining plant here in Tailem Bend that had begun sending water to the south-east. O'Grady said there was so much more being taken out than was being put back that he didn't know where it would end. 'Adelaide has double the population it had ten years ago and towns near here are growing as well; heaps more people and no more water.'

The punt man used to live near the punt; the wharf was where kids swam and jumped off. Now there are fewer kids and no wharf. Now there was only a punt man who lived out of town and the jetty was a collection of old wooden posts that had been fenced off with signs warning of the danger.

The river looked weary, as though it could do nothing more. If it was youthful near Bringenbrong and middle-aged at Swan Hill, then near Renmark and Berri, even down to Morgan, it had been showing the renewed enthusiasm of approaching retirement.

After a couple of hours of talking to the locals in the bar, I walked down to the tinnie and sat for a while in the dark. The wind had dropped and the night was still. The cool change was welcome although it was strange to be cold after a few weeks of heat. In the heavens a large blurred ring circled the moon; there were no stars. Whispering so no one else could hear me, I told the river that it was nearly over; that we were both coming to the end of our journey.

The night was spent being woken regularly by the constant stream of trucks that roared up and down the highway, and very early next morning, on the way down to load the tinnie,

I encountered two blokes who had been in the bar the night before.

Paul was a short but rather wide man. Grey hair hung over his shoulders and his equally grey beard was thick and long, coming to a point almost at his chest. His mate Charlie was a small olive-skinned man of Maltese descent, the first of his family to be born in Australia. The pair were working on a dairy farm on the other side of the river, putting in pipes to make it comply with the new government regulations that stated there was to be no water returned to the river from dairy farms. Deposits left by cows combined with rain and irrigation of their pastures meant excess nutrients were washed back into the river, causing problems for drinking water and for fish. And it was not only animal waste products, there were also fertilisers and chemicals used by farmers. The farm's plan was to have a pipeline in front of the levee bank as well as lasered run-off from the paddocks. The water would be collected in a pond and pumped through the pipe back up to the farm and recycled.

Paul said there were benefits everywhere. 'The river is healthier, it loses less water and the farmers save money on both water and fertiliser.'

Paul was an articulate advocate for the changes. He rubbed his hands through his magnificently cultured whiskers. 'We live in the driest state in the driest country on the driest continent,' he said. 'Basically, this is the only river we have in this state.'

As the men left for work they told me that every dairy farm had to comply with the legislation within the next few years. Typically, said Paul, 'some are enthusiastic about it and others are being bloody stupid'.

In the late 1800s, South Australia was thrown into disarray by the departure of men to the Victorian goldfields, leaving behind debts and families with no support. The Commissioner of Police, Alexander Tolmer, decided to take a troop of men to retrieve the gold dug by these miners and return it to those who were in need. Wellington was where they crossed the river, and the troops eventually brought back what amounted to millions of pounds worth of the precious metal.

I, too, was going to cross the river at Wellington—with Garry Dodd, the ferry man. He assured me the tinnie would be safe if I wanted to make a crossing or two with him.

Garry was a fourth-generation river man and had worked on the PS *Coonawarra* for a year while completing his matriculation by correspondence. Then he had lived in Murray Bridge for twenty years on an old wool barge called the *Alfred* which his grandfather had built the superstructure for.

Garry's great-grandfather, Ebenezer, had captained steamers on the river. His grandfather, Charlie, once owned the slipway at Mannum and, at about the same time, Charlie's brother Ainsworth had owned the slipway at Goolwa.

As a milk truck crept gingerly off the ferry so as not to wobble it too much, Garry said that, to him, Wellington was a place where all the goodness of the river came together. 'It's almost the finish, nice and quiet and peaceful. Good river, good people.'

In 1846 the first hand-cranked ferry on the river was established at Wellington, followed in 1914 by the first power-driven one. The lot of a ferryman, as diverse as it is, hadn't changed much. Garry admitted wryly that waving at every vehicle when they drove onto the ferry and then again when they rolled off meant that his arms were in the air most of the day.

After four crossings with Garry—two over and two back—the tinnie and I headed off to Brinkley, four kilometres away towards Lake Alexandrina and the last place on the river.

The water around Wellington was reputed to be rough when the southerly winds blew but today it was perfect. The sun was on my back, the heat tolerable and the last of the river proper in front of me. As the river became wider and wider, I turned back. As the old fisherman's prayer went, 'Protect me my Lord; my boat is so small and your sea is so large.' Even if this wasn't the sea the message was still relevant. Charles Sturt was braver than me. When he saw the lake he simply ordered his men to row across it, naming it after Alexandrina, the princess who was to become Queen Victoria.

An hour later, back at Wellington, there was a touch of sadness in loading the tinnie for the last time; we had become quite attached to each other. After making sure it was secure, I ran my hand gently down the side, thanking it for looking after me on our many trips, then jumped in the ute and drove round to Goolwa.

End of summer

Goolwa—the river meets the sea

The Murray made its way across the bottom of Lake Alexandrina to emerge once more as a river. The small town of Milang is on the edge of the lake but it was not until the town of Clayton that the river regained the identity lost at Wellington. Clayton was the last place riverboat captains stopped after leaving Goolwa. Inclement weather would usually cause them to stay overnight before attempting the lake crossing. Foolhardy souls attempted to cross in rough weather but soon turned back. All the old captains had problems with the lake. Crossing the lake in good weather would only take a few hours but it wasn't always easy. In bad weather it became downright hazardous.

After Point Sturt, the Finnis River and Currency Creek join the Murray before a wide sweeping bend takes it past Hindmarsh Island and towards the sea. Hindmarsh is a name with which Australians are familiar.

The Hindmarsh Island affair, as it was known, began in the 1990s when a bridge to replace the ferry across the river from

Goolwa was planned to help with the commercial development of a marina. Initially the plan didn't include a bridge, but permission to build was rejected unless one was added. The marina owners had to pay for the bridge's construction, but when they ran into financial trouble, the state government became involved, guaranteeing the bridge would go ahead.

As plans were nearing completion and the first sod was to be turned, a group of Ngarrindjeri women claimed the island was special to them. This was 'secret women's business', and none of it could be revealed. The women's objection was upheld and the bridge was banned. Then another group of women from the same clan claimed that it was all a hoax. A Royal Commission confirmed their assertion and the bridge was built. Opinions as to who was right and who was wrong abounded, but the one thing for certain was that the bridge was constructed, the white folks on the island built their marina, and they became very, very rich.

It was near Hindmarsh Island that Sturt had an altercation with Aborigines after he found the channel that would lead him to the sea. A number of the locals gathered on the shore and, with spears at the ready, a few made their way into the water. When Sturt picked up a gun the Aborigines recognised what he had and ran back up the beach quickly. Sturt laid his weapon down and continued his journey. The crew then tried to row through the mouth of the river into the sea, but all attempts failed as the sea lifted them up and threw them back each time.

In vain Sturt and his party searched for ships that might have been able to take them back to Sydney. Instead, they were resigned to rowing back the way they had come. If their meagre rations were to last the distance, they had to complete the journey in the same time, only this time rowing upstream against the current, and with no help from the sails.

The crew had taken twenty-six days to row down the Murray and, weak from hunger, they took only twenty-three days to return to the Murrumbidgee junction. Seven days later, dropping from exhaustion and pain from the never-ending pulling against the current of the flooded river, they reached their camp at Maude—but found it deserted. Seventeen days after that they arrived at Narrandera, where Sturt pitched camp and ordered two of his men to go for help. It arrived on the day the rations ran out. One of the men went insane as a result of the trip, and Sturt became blind, staying that way for several months and suffering eye problems for the rest of his life. Eight years later he completed his Murray River exploration from the point where Hume and Hovell started to where he had first found the Murray—the Murrumbidgee junction.

After Sturt completed his trip there was a feeling that a settlement should be established near the mouth of the river so the inland could be opened up. Captain William Light inspected the area but said that the mouth of the river was not navigable, an opinion with which Sturt agreed. Light then headed elsewhere and founded Adelaide.

However the Murray River was still on the minds of some and soon Goolwa was established as the final point for river shipping. Goolwa means 'elbow' in the local Ngarrindjeri language and during a survey in the 1840s the place was called 'Town on the Goolwa'. Later it became Port Pullen before reverting to plain Goolwa.

Although only a few kilometres from the sea, Goolwa became the first inland port in Australia, with four river companies establishing themselves and building as many as twenty-seven steamers and twenty-two barges at the local ship-yards. At its peak, during the 1880s, about 25 000 bales of wool passed through the wharf each year, with as many as 89 000 in one year.

In 1857 a huge mast was built on Barker's Knoll on the Coorong side of the Murray mouth. Here flags were flown to warn riverboat captains whether or not the mouth was navigable. Another was put up in 1879 on high ground behind the wharf, where the flags were then conveyed to signal to captains coming across the lake.

Francis Cadell traded through the mouth for a number of years bringing wool from distances of up to 3500 river kilometres. But with the success of the river trade, jealousy broke out. Towns in both South Australia and Victoria—Echuca and Morgan in particular—soon had railways arriving and, even though it took a few years, Goolwa's importance dissipated. Roads were constructed to the ocean port of Port Elliot, where inland produce could be transferred directly to ships that would take it around to Adelaide, up to Melbourne or Sydney and, sometimes, throughout the world. Many ships were lost off the coast at Port Elliot, so eventually attention then turned to Victor Harbor. Goolwa was meant to be the New Orleans of Australia, the Murray our own Mississippi. Neither eventuated.

Kendall Jones met me as he returned from attempting to check out a couple of the lake's beacons he was asked to look after. 'Bit too windy today, bit dangerous out there.'

With a few rivets that needed replacing and a few dents that needed beating out, his boat was at the opposite end of the nautical scale to the *Coorong Wanderer*, the vessel he'd been in when I met him at Euston. I was glad to see Kendall and Roma again, they had sense of pragmatism not often found on either side of the river debate.

'It's stuffed in places,' said Kendall, 'but not half as stuffed as some people think—and not half as stuffed as it's goin' to be if they don't fix things.'

During lunch—a freshly caught crab each, with Roma's delicious homemade seafood sauce—Kendall said that the river had had more reports written about it than anything else on earth. 'They've been talking about it and reporting about it forever. If you laid 'em all end to end they'd cover the length of the river, I reckon.'

Throwing away the towel on which we'd wiped our hands, Kendall suggested we take a tour of the town. After a few slow circuits of the main streets we drove across the bridge to Hindmarsh Island. Even though he was not sure about the Aboriginal claims, Kendall mentioned that the owners of the marina were not too popular with the locals. 'Lots of people have done things they shouldn't be too proud of.'

The marina and its associated housing development was the biggest in the Southern Hemisphere, with grand, ultra-expensive houses either built or being built everywhere you looked. Canals filled with water diverted from the Murray snaked past each house and on every block, whether it had been built on or not, a pontoon stood waiting for the new owners and their boats.

A few minutes later we parked near the Goolwa Barrage. When the river leaves Lake Alexandrina it takes five channels, all with barrages. The purpose of the barrages is to separate salt water from the river and to stabilise river levels upstream. Each barrage is fitted with stoplogs that are put in and taken out depending on the water levels. During floods the stoplogs are taken out completely, while during periods of low rivers they must all be in place to stop the flow out and to keep the lake levels as high as possible. Water level upstream is normally kept about .75 of a metre above sea level.

Back in town and driving towards the beach, Kendall told me about steamers going out the mouth and around to Victor Harbor before the railway came, describing how they'd struggle to get through the mouth with the sea roaring in their faces. In his thirty-odd years in Goolwa and with his extensive knowledge of the waters, Kendall had only seen a few boats going out and had never got out himself, despite many attempts.

One of the earliest known experiences at the mouth was that of a Captain Blenkinsop and his crew in 1837 in their whaleboat the *Currency Creek*. The boat was carted by bullock dray to within a few kilometres of the mouth, after which it was rowed successfully through the water to the open sea. A few days later Sir John Jeffcote, who had been wrecked at Rosetta Bay, accompanied by Blenkinsop and four other men, tried to repeat the feat.

The breakers were much bigger and stronger and, although they almost got through, the whaleboat was soon overturned. Blenkinsop, Jeffcote and two of the crew were drowned. The survivors were dragged to shore by Aborigines who had watched it all unfold. Blenkinsop's was the only body recovered. They buried him the next day with the broken whaleboat placed over his body.

Now there was just one thing left to do and Kendall's four-wheel drive clambered over the rolling sand dunes as we headed down the beach. He glanced across at me watching the sea apprehensively.

'Ready for this?' he asked.

I wasn't sure.

A large sign at the entrance to the beach warned of the danger of proceeding without the appropriate vehicle. In large letters it said that anyone who drove down the beach and became bogged would have to wait for help and then pay all costs associated with being taken out. Kendall said there had been a few cars lost when they became stranded and the tide came in and swamped them. 'Silly bastards shouldn't be there anyway.'

We bounced down the beach, swaying around patches of seaweed and dipping suddenly as we crossed channels left empty by the receding tide. Sand dunes on our left baked in the sun while their sandy tops were whisked away in the wind. I'd started my journey at the other end of the river in a four-wheel drive and would finish in the same way.

As we climbed a sand dune, we could see two dredges hard at work in the distance. Kendall stopped where two large black pipes spewed water and sand together onto the dune. 'This is where those dredges send it.' He shook his head. Eventually the tide would wash away the base of the dune causing the sand on the top to soon be back on the beach. It would then wash back into the sea and the sea, in turn, would sweep it back into the mouth where the dredges would begin the whole process again.

A nice contract, said Kendall, one that didn't have an end date; if they kept pumping onto the beach, then it would just go on and on. 'Seems a bit stupid to put it there when there are plenty of places where it could be put to advantage.'

From the top of the dune, the Coorong stretched away into the distance. Here, salinity levels had reached three times that of sea water and bird and plant life was substantially diminished. Pelicans, once part of the largest colony in the country, had not bred for four years and migratory bird numbers had dropped from 250 000 in the 1960s to just 50 000. Fish species were disappearing regularly. The Coorong was in desperate need of water.

Back in the passenger's seat I stared out the window at the stupidity of the dredges and the sad, almost aching, Coorong. Kendall started the motor and five minutes later we pulled up on the flat sand where the Murray, exhausted, joined the sea. Breakers thundered towards the river somewhere deep below, trying desperately to escape. Roma had said that on occasions she could see the spread of river soil out to sea, a big dark patch that meant the river was in charge. Now there was no flow, and hadn't been for some time. Now the river simply obeyed instructions from dredges and stoplogs and barrages and locks and weirs and mankind.

Kendall leant against the vehicle and watched me walk towards the water. I considered swimming but thought that presumptuous. Instead, wading out waist deep I felt the surge of the ages as the clean, vibrant Southern Ocean rolled towards me. Across the waves, the sky met the sea in an expanse of vivid blue spattered by clouds as soft as handfuls of cotton wool. Gulls appeared to make no headway as they toiled above, their cries echoing through the sound of the wind.

Back on the sand I picked up a shell and a striped rock, fingering them gently. It had come to this. A man and a journey, both now irrelevant as my travelling companion became anonymous in the ocean.

I hoped the river felt like me. That amid the sadness there was still a sense of completion, a sense of finality; a sense of wonder.

Looking to the horizon I wondered about the water that had oozed from the ground the summer before. Had it been wasted, dried up, turned to salt? Or had it survived, flowed through the mayhem and loneliness that was the river and disappeared, unlamented, unloved, out through this place into the unknown?

Quietly, I thanked the river for its company then, a richer man, turned and headed home.

Acknowledgments

There are so many people to thank, so many who gave freely of themselves; so many who took the time to talk and encourage me during my journey. Many of us were not officially introduced and so you are therefore nameless, but my thanks go to you anyway.

I am particularly grateful to Stefano de Pieri for his help, friendship and for his wonderful Foreword. Also for encouraging me with his passion for all things river and culinary.

Thanks also to Paul Kane for permission to publish his poem.

Another big thank you goes to Stuart Carless for the photographs that grace the front and back covers.

My old friend Ted Ward was a great help to me (although not to my wellbeing) and, as humble as it might be, the Iron Dry is a boat to rank with the best that have travelled the river.

Richard Hubbard guided me to the source of the Murray and through his generosity showed me places I would never otherwise have seen.

Col Walker gave me an insight into his people and his beliefs that were an inspiration to me and should be an inspiration to all.

The lifelong riverman, Bill Hogg, and his stories of the river and his father, Paddy, have their own place in history and I am privileged to know them.

Peter Koetsveld was also a big help in patiently making me understand more about the river and its waters.

The river travellers, Kendell and Roma Jones, welcomed me into their homes on land and water and gave me a sense of the river at its end.

The amazing Johnny Gurr is a woman whose passion and love for the Murray rubbed off on me.

Old navy mates, Dave Turnbull and Alan Stevens, as well as jogging my memory for things long forgotten, explained their feelings for the river clearly.

Rose Kemp and Sam Fielke made my river dining experience one to remember.

Ray Weedon showed me how the biggest boat of all travelled the river and also how there are some who don't yet understand how fragile the Murray has become.

Others to thank include Tammy Van Wisse, Alf Wilson, Betty Walton, Andrew Millar, Rex Beaver, Peter Sutherland, Ian Douglas, 'Tippy' Lean, Benita Lamond, Jules the Muse, Neil Hutchinson and Gary Aitken, Rose Williams, Tim Edmonds, Jim Brooks, Leon Fielke, Bill Moularadellis, Omer Najar, Ron Simpfendorfer and Garry Dodd.

A big thanks also to four people who drive me mad yet at the same time keep me sane—Grumpy, Precious, Goolia and Boris (in no particular order).

Of course the book would not have seen the light of day without the continuing support of Rebecca Kaiser at Allen & Unwin. Thanks also to my editor, Jeanmarie Morosin, who looks after everything so well and to Ali Lavau for her sensitive copy-editing.

My journey was made a lot easier through the use of *River Murray Charts* by Maureen Wright; *Murray River Pilot* by Ronald and Margaret Baker; and *River of Islands* by Kath and Leon Bentley.

Other information was gathered from newspapers including *The Age*; *The Australian*; the *Herald-Sun*; the *Adelaide Advertiser*; the *Riverine Herald*, Echuca; *The Guardian*, Swan Hill; *The Border-Mail*, Albury.

Books I read and gathered information from—deliberately or inadvertently—included *Australia's Great River* by R.M. Younger (Horizon Publishing 1976); *The Murray River* by Amanda Burton (Australian Geographic 2000); *The Murray, a River and its People* by Paul Sinclair (Melbourne University Press 2001); *Australia's Greatest River* by John Larkins and Steve Parish (Rigby 1982); *Ancestral Streams* by Danny O'Neil (Bookhenge 2005); *Water into Gold* by Ernest Hill (Robertson and Mullens 1938); *River Boats* by Ian Mudie (Rigby 1961); *River Rovers* by EJ Brady (Roberston and Co 1911); *Tracks* by Max Jones (1981); *Messing About In Boats* by YM Johnson (Gurr 1992); *A River Woman* by Pearl Woman (Southern Cross University Press 2001). I also used some of the information about Aboriginal life that an old family friend Derek French sent me.

The Internet was also a source of information including the valuable websites: <www.mdbc.com.au>, <www.savethe murray.com.au> www.murrayriver.com.au>.

Many brochures picked up from Information Centres along the river were useful and many of them are also published on the Internet. All were a great help.

If I have missed anyone or anything then please accept my apology and know that I am grateful to you all.

The Slow River Movement

The Slow River Movement transcends traditional state borders and is a campaign designed to promote the food and wine industry along the entire length of Australia's greatest river and undisputed food bowl—the Murray.

The Slow River Movement is at the heart of a wide reaching strategy, inspired by the International Slow Food Movement, that recognises the growing desire for visitors to the Murray River to savour and appreciate food and wine that has been produced in a responsible manner and then prepared for the plate with passion.

The movement puts the produce of the river on the world stage, while also contributing to the river's health and providing much needed professional assistance to emerging industry talent.

The Slow River Movement also includes a range of support projects, including:

- the Chefs of the Murray program
- participation in select consumer and trade food and wine shows
- development of a touring guide featuring the Murray's food and wine industry
- development of a Murray River Food and Wine calendar
- a national promotional program identifying the river's local cultural, food and wine events and festivals.